FOUNDATIONS OF

BIBLICAL RESTORATION

Scriptural Authority, Canon, and the Restoration of Yada' Yahuah

MBRS Book 1 — Associate-Level Foundations

The Official Student Textbook

DR. YERAL E. OGANDO

FOUNDATIONS OF BIBLICAL RESTORATION

The Official Student Textbook for the Master of Biblical Restoration Studies (MBRS)
By
Dr. Yeral E. Ogando

Authored and published by
Dr. Yeral E. Ogando
Adopted for instructional use by
Yahuah Institute of Biblical Restoration, Inc.
As the core text for
The Master of Biblical Restoration Studies (MBRS) Program

Scripture quotations are taken exclusively from Dabar Yahuah Scriptures – www.yahuahbible.com. This textbook is produced for academic, instructional, and theological training purposes within the MBRS program and affiliated courses.
"All instructional texts used by the MBRS Program are independently authored and published by Dr. Yeral E. Ogando. The Institute adopts these texts solely for instructional purposes and does not own, publish, or receive revenue from them."

ISBN: 978-1-946249-41-8

1. AUTHORIZATION & INSTITUTIONAL STATEMENT

This textbook, Foundations of Biblical Restoration, is authored and published by Dr. Yeral E. Ogando and is adopted and approved for instructional use by Yahuah Institute of Biblical Restoration, Inc. as the core instructional text for the Master of Biblical Restoration Studies (MBRS) program.

All doctrinal positions, terminology, instructional structures, and evaluative standards contained within this volume are governed exclusively by Dabar Yahuah Scriptures as preserved in the Scriptures recognized by the Institute: the inspired writings of the Tanakh (Old Testament), the preserved Apokryfos, and the Renewed Covenant (New Testament) writings.

This text operates within a closed canonical and theological framework for the academic cycle in which it is issued. No external denominational systems, philosophical methodologies, speculative Yada Yahuah (theology), or institutional traditions are permitted to govern interpretation, instruction, or assessment within the MBRS program.

This Student Edition is authorized for instructional use solely within the MBRS program.

Unauthorized reproduction, distribution, or use outside of Institute-approved instructional contexts is prohibited.

2. PREFACE & STATEMENT OF PURPOSE

Foundations of Biblical Restoration exists because Scripture itself demands restoration.

This textbook was not written to defend denominational systems, preserve inherited theology, or harmonize philosophical frameworks with Scripture. It was written to allow **Dabar Yahuah** to govern Yada Yahuah (theology) without competition.

Modern theology often begins with assumptions and searches Scripture for support. Restoration Yada Yahuah (theology) reverses that order. Scripture establishes authority, defines categories, diagnoses corruption, and reveals restoration according to divine intent rather than human tradition.

This book serves as the **single, integrated instructional text** for the Master of Biblical Restoration Studies (MBRS). It guides the student from Scriptural Witness through, *Yahuah: Restoration Guide,* the ***Origin of Evil:*** *Biblical Truths Hidden in Plain Sight,* the **Three Humanities™**: *The Division of Humanity in Yahuah's Plan* - Volume 1, and th***e*** ***Three Humanities™***: *The Restoration of the First Humanity in Yahuah's Plan*—culminating in independent thesis defense.

3. STATEMENT OF PURPOSE

The purpose of this textbook is to:

> Establish Scripture as the sole governing authority
> Restore biblical categories obscured by tradition and translation
> Define evil without attributing corruption to Yahuah
> Explain humanity through the **Three Humanities™** framework
> Present restoration as transformation, not repair
> Prepare students to defend **Restoration Yada Yahuah** (theology)

independently and accurately

This text is not devotional. It is not speculative. It is instructional, corrective, and authoritative.

4. PROGRAM LEARNING OUTCOMES
MASTER OF BIBLICAL RESTORATION STUDIES (MBRS)

Upon successful completion of the MBRS program, the student will be able to:

1.Demonstrate Covenantal Reasoning across the full body of Scripture, integrating the Tanakh (Old Testament), Apokryfos, and Renewed Covenant (New Testament) writings without contradiction.

2.Explain Scriptural authority as divinely originated, canonically bounded, and covenantal preserved.

3.Define evil, corruption, judgment, and restoration using Scriptural categories alone, without reliance on philosophical or denominational frameworks.

4.Articulate the Three Humanities™ framework (First, Second, Third Humanities and the Variant) using Scripture-governed anthropology and lineage Yada Yahuah (theology).

5.Distinguish between sin, corruption, and Creational alteration, explaining why restoration requires transformation rather than moral repair.

6.Apply covenant language discipline responsibly, demonstrating how words govern doctrine and prevent theological distortion.

7.Defend Restoration Yada Yahuah (theology) from creation to consummation as a unified, Scripture-consistent system.

8.Produce and defend a master-level thesis grounded exclusively in Scripture, demonstrating doctrinal clarity, canonical consistency, and methodological integrity.

5. HOW TO USE THIS TEXTBOOK

This textbook is designed for **structured, sequential use** within the MBRS program.

STUDENT RESPONSIBILITIES

- Read all assigned Scripture before engaging commentary or explanations.
- Follow the progression of weeks and months without skipping sections.
- Use only Institute-approved Scriptural sources when completing assignments.
- Adhere strictly to locked templates, prompts, and evaluation criteria.

- Demonstrate mastery through clarity, Scripture use, and disciplined reasoning.

INSTRUCTIONAL STRUCTURE

- Each Term builds upon previous authority and doctrine.
- Each Month introduces defined instructional goals.
- Each Week focuses on specific Scriptural concepts.
- Assessments measure integration and reasoning, not memorization.

This text is not designed for casual reading.
It is designed for **formation, correction, and qualification.**

Students who attempt to bypass structure, introduce external systems, or rely on speculation will not advance.

6. ACADEMIC & SCRIPTURAL INTEGRITY STATEMENT

Enrollment in the MBRS program constitutes agreement to the following standards:
- **Scripture governs all conclusions.**
- **Dabar Yahuah is the highest authority.**
- No denominational, philosophical, or speculative systems may override Scripture.
- All work must be original, truthful, and accurately cited.
- Plagiarism, doctrinal innovation, or misrepresentation of Scripture results in disqualification.
- Advancement is evaluative, not automatic.

This program values **clarity over creativity, submission over speculation, and truth over tradition.**

The goal is not affirmation, but formation.

Authorized Textual Resources and Access

The instructional texts and Scriptural resources referenced within the Master of Biblical Restoration Studies (MBRS) program are made available through designated platforms.

Primary reference texts and supporting source materials authored by Dr. Yeral E. Ogando are openly accessible at www.yahuahdabar.com. These materials may be read online by any visitor. Registration allows users to download PDF versions of the source texts. These materials are publicly available and are not restricted to enrolled students.

The Dabar Yahuah Scriptures, including the Tanakh (Old Testament), Apokryfos, and Renewed Covenant (New Testament) writings, are openly accessible for online reading at www.yahuahbible.com. These texts are provided as the authorized Scriptural reference for the MBRS program and are available to all readers.

For Scriptural study and term-level consultation, students are instructed to use the Dabar Yahuah Scriptures App, including its Strong Concordance tools for Hebrew and Greek reference. This tool is used for confirming word forms, meanings, and Scriptural usage in alignment with the Institute's instructional framework.

The Student Edition textbooks, however, are not publicly distributed through these websites. Student textbooks are provided through the Institute's instructional platform or authorized course distribution channels, with the exception of the Amazon print edition.

These access distinctions are intentional and form part of the Institute's instructional and evaluative framework.

FROM THEOLOGY TO YĀDAʿ YAHUAH

Why the Yahuah Institute of Biblical Restoration, Inc. Rejects the term "Theology" and Restores Biblical Knowing

1. INTRODUCTION

The Yahuah Institute of Biblical Restoration, Inc. is committed to restoring biblical truth to its original covenantal framework. This commitment requires not only the restoration of doctrine, but also the restoration of language, method, and authority.

One of the most fundamental restorations we make is the deliberate rejection of the term "theology" and its replacement with the biblical concept of Yādaʿ Yahuah.

This decision is not stylistic, cultural, or reactionary.

It is linguistic, biblical, and doctrinally necessary.

2. THE ORIGIN OF THE TERM "THEOLOGY"

The English word theology derives from the Greek term θεολογία (theologia), formed from:

- θεός (theos) — god
- λογία (logia / logos) — discourse, reasoning, philosophical inquiry

Historically, theologia meant "reasoned discourse about the gods."

It originated in Greek philosophical thought, not in Scripture.

This term was later imposed upon biblical studies during the Hellenistic and post-Constantinian periods, when Greek philosophical categories were used to systematize biblical texts.

Biblical authors never used this term.

They never described their writings, teachings, or revelations as "theology."

3. WHY "THEOLOGY" IS INCOMPATIBLE WITH SCRIPTURE

The concept of theology assumes:

- that Elohiym (God) is an object of analysis,
- that truth is reached through intellectual reasoning,
- and that humans define knowledge about Elohiym (God).

Scripture presents the opposite order:
- Yahuah reveals,
- humanity receives,
- knowledge flows from obedience and covenant relationship.

Theological systems frequently place human reason as the organizing authority over revelation.
Scripture places revelation above human reason.

For this reason, theology is not a neutral term — it is a foreign philosophical framework imposed upon biblical revelation.

4. HEBREW DOES NOT THINK IN "-OLOGY" CATEGORIES

Hebrew biblical thought does not begin with abstract nouns or speculative systems.
It begins with verbs, action, and relationship.
Greek thought is:
> abstract
> analytical
> speculative

Hebrew thought is:
> relational
> covenantal
> revealed
> lived and obeyed

Therefore, the question is not: "What is the Hebrew word for theology?"
The correct question is: "How does Scripture define knowing Yahuah?"

5. THE BIBLICAL ROOT: יָדַע (YĀDAʿ)

The foundational biblical term is the Hebrew verb יָדַע (Yādaʿ).

Yādaʿ means:

> to know relationally
>
> to know experientially
>
> to know covenantal
>
> to know through obedience and encounter

This is not theoretical knowledge.

Scriptural Examples:

> Genesis 4:1 — "Adam knew Eve"
>
> Exodus 33:12 — "I know you by name"
>
> Jeremiah 31:34 — "They shall all know Me"

In every case, knowing is relational and experiential, not informational.

6. DAʿAT (דַּעַת) DEPENDS ON YĀDAʿ

The noun דַּעַת (Daʿat) — "knowledge" — is derived from Yādaʿ.

This means:

> Daʿat is the result of knowing,
>
> not the source of knowing.

When Daʿat is detached from Yādaʿ, knowledge becomes abstract and distorted — exactly what occurs in theological systems.

Scripture never treats knowledge as an independent intellectual possession.

Knowledge is always the fruit of covenant relationship.

7. THE RESTORED BIBLICAL FRAMEWORK: YADA YAHUAH

For this reason, the Institute restores the biblical category:

יָדַע יְהוָה —Yādaʿ Yahuah

"To know Yahuah by covenantal revelation and obedience."

Formal Definition:

Yādaʿ Yahuah is the covenantal act of knowing Yahuah through His self-revelation, instruction, and lived obedience. It is not speculative reasoning about

Elohiym (God), but relational knowing grounded in faithfulness, encounter, and submission to His Word.

Daʿat Yahuah (the knowledge of Yahuah) is the outcome of Yādaʿ, not its substitute.

8. IMPLICATIONS FOR EDUCATION AND DEGREES

Because of this restoration:

> We do not teach theology

> We restore Yāda-ʿbased covenant knowledge

> Our programs form servants, not analysts

> Our degrees represent covenantal responsibility and accountability, not merely intellectual status

The Institute rejects Greek philosophical abstraction in favor of biblical revelation.

9. CONCLUSION

The restoration of truth requires the restoration of language.

Theology is not a biblical category.

Yādaʿ Yahuah is.

By restoring Yāda ʿYahuah, the Institute aligns itself with:

> Scripture's authority,

> covenantal knowing,

> and the original biblical worldview.

This restoration is not optional. It is foundational.

OFFICIAL STATEMENT

"We do not reason about Yahuah; we know Him as He reveals Himself."

Contents

LEARNING GUIDE - OFFICIAL STUDENT TEXT BOOK

MASTER-LEVEL ECCLESIASTICAL DEGREE PROGRAM
(Faith-Based, Non-Accredited)
Yahuah Institute of Biblical Restoration, Inc.

TERM I — FOUNDATIONS OF CANON & RESTORATION

Stage I of the Master-Level Ecclesiastical Degree Program
(Faith-Based, Non-Accredited)
Associate-Level Foundations · Months 1–4

ACADEMIC ORIENTATION — TERM I · MONTH 1

This term marks the student's entry into the first stage of the Master-level program of the Yahuah Institute of Biblical Restoration, Inc.. While this program is ecclesiastical and non-accredited, it is structured with academic rigor and disciplinary expectations consistent with advanced biblical study.

Term I (Months 1-4) functions as the Associate-Level foundation of the program. During this stage, students are trained in the essential principles of Scriptural Witness, Scriptural preservation, covenantal continuity, and restored Yadaʿ Yahuah methodology. Advancement beyond this stage is conditional upon demonstrated mastery.

This course is designed for disciplined, text-centered study at a university level. Students are expected to engage Scripture directly, prioritize internal Scriptural testimony, and evaluate authority structures based on covenantal appointment rather than later institutional tradition.

This Institute does not approach Scripture devotionally or denominationally. Instead, it employs a restorative covenantal methodology, which examines divine instruction according to origin, preservation, transmission, and guardianship as revealed within Scripture itself.

Students are expected to:

> Read primary texts carefully and contextually

> Distinguish between divine origin and human transmission

> Suspend inherited theological assumptions while engaging the material

> Demonstrate comprehension through Scriptural reasoning rather than opinion

Disagreement is not penalized; unsupported assertion is. All conclusions must be traceable to **Dabar Yahuah** as presented in Scripture.

TERM I - MONTH 1
MODULE 1 OVERVIEW

• *Methodological Framework of This Module*

This module operates under the following interpretive principles:

1.Covenantal Authority Supersedes Institutional Authority
Divine instruction is evaluated based on covenantal appointment and Scriptural testimony, not later ecclesiastical decisions or councils.

2.Origin Precedes Textual Form
Written Scripture is understood as transmission, not origin. Authority is traced to Yahuah Himself rather than to manuscripts, languages, or compilations.

3.Heaven-to-Earth Flow of Instruction
Instruction originates with Yahuah, is preserved in heaven, and is transmitted to earth through appointed means. Authority never flows in the reverse direction.

4.Internal Scriptural Consistency
Scripture is interpreted using Scripture. External theological systems are not treated as interpretive authorities.

5.Restorative, Not Progressive, Interpretation
Later revelation restores clarity; it does not replace, revise, or negate earlier divine instruction.
This framework governs all readings, discussions, and evaluations throughout Term I.

This module teaches how Scripture defines itself, where it comes from, and why it holds supreme authority over Yada Yahuah (theology), tradition, and doctrine. You will study Scripture as divine instruction, originating with Yahuah, preserved through appointed guardians, and recorded according to heavenly testimony.

TERM I - MONTH 1 - WEEK 1 — SCRIPTURE FROM THE BEGINNING
INTRODUCTION TO MODULE 1

The Scriptures are the divine word and Dabar of Yahuah, where he expresses his thoughts and will for his master creation, humanity.

Let us first define and understand the meaning of the word "Scriptures"

It is the set of books, teachings and practices given by Yahuah and taught by his people; it consist of all the books of the Old testament (those that are inspired), all the books of the Apokryfos (those that are inspired) and all the books of the New Testaments (those that are inspired). Nothing outside of these three canons constitute a law for Yahuah's people, because it is outside of the Scriptures.

We need to understand that the word scripture itself is just a translation that we have inherited from the Latin language; however, the real origine and correct word is dâbâr (דָּבָר), which literally means word, book, chronicles, commandment, decree, deed, message. These are only the main meanings of the word Dabar "Debārīm (Deuteronomy) 30:14".

We will be using the word Dabar in most of the cases, which is the Hebrew restored term. Therefore, Dabar: is the word of Yahuah (Dabar Yahuah), his commandments, teachings and decrees for us.

You will study **Dabar Yahuah** as the divine instruction, originating with Yahuah, preserved through appointed guardians, and recorded according to heavenly testimony.

MODULE 1 LEARNING OUTCOMES

By the end of Term I – Month 1, students should be able to:

- Distinguish between the **origin, preservation**, and **transmission** of Dabar Yahuah
- Demonstrate from Scripture that divine instruction predates Sinai and written codification

- Explain the concept of **Heavenly Tablets** and their relationship to earthly instruction
- Identify the difference between **Tôrâh** as divine instruction and **canon** as human classification
- Trace Scriptural guardianship of Tôrâh through covenantal appointment rather than institutional authority
- Evaluate tradition, doctrine, and theology against Dabar Yahuah using Scriptural reasoning
- Mastery is demonstrated through accurate Scriptural citation, logical coherence, and covenantal consistency.

TERM I - MONTH 1 - WEEK 1 - READINGS:
WEEK 1 LEARNING OUTCOMES — SCRIPTURE FROM THE BEGINNING

By the end of Week 1, students should be able to:
- Explain **Dabar Yahuah** as the origin of creation and instruction
- Identify commandment and accountability prior to Sinai
- Distinguish divine origin from later textual recording
- Support conclusions using Scriptural examples from creation narratives and pre-Sinai accounts

Read Chapter 1 from *Yahuah: Restoration Guide.*
Watch the given videos for supplement tools and support.

CHAPTER 1 READING SCOPE — WHAT TO EXTRACT

As you read Chapter 1 from Yahuah: Restoration Guide, your objective is not to master every subject introduced in the chapter. Chapter 1 contains multiple themes that will be addressed later in this term and in future modules. For this week, your task is to extract only what directly supports the foundation of

Scripture as divinely originated instruction.

Read Chapter 1 with the following focus:

Dabar at Creation (Origin of Instruction)

Identify how creation itself is established by command and decree, not by process or human explanation. Observe that Dabar precedes form, life, and order, demonstrating that divine instruction existed before humanity and before any written codification.

The First Commandment and the Definition of Sin

From the Garden of Eden account, identify the first commandment given to humanity and how Scripture defines sin as **disobedience** to **Dabar**. Note that authority and instruction exist prior to transgression, and that death enters as a result of rejecting commandment.

Early Record and Heavenly Testimony

Pay close attention to references involving Chănôk (Enoch) and Yôbêl (Jubilees), writing, testimony, seasons, and revelation. Identify how Scripture presents early recording, instruction, and heavenly witness as part of divine order long before Mosheh.

Pre-Sinai Continuity of Instruction

Observe how instruction, law, accountability, and covenant responsibility exist before Sinai. Note that what later becomes codified through Mosheh already existed in practice, order, and expectation.

Chapter 1 also introduces additional subjects—such as the Watchers, Nephilim, demons, the Tower of Babel, and Sedôm and Ămôrâh. These subjects are not the focus of Week 1 unless explicitly assigned by your instructor at a later time. For this week, acknowledge their presence without attempting to systematize them. Your goal in reading Chapter 1 is to confirm—by Scripture—that **Dabar Yahuah originates with Yahuah from Creation**, that commandment exists prior to Sinai, and that Scripture is transmitted through divine instruction rather than human tradition.

TERM I - MONTH 1 - WEEK 1 - READINGS 2:

- **Bereshith 1:1–3:** These are the first words found in Dabar Yahuah and they come as reflection to show the beginning of everything originated directly by the Dabar of Yahuah.
- **Bereshith 2:16–17:** Here you can clearly see how Yahuah gave commandments to Adam and that his Dabar was from the very beginning, thus showing humanity with Dabar from very first day.
- **Jubilees 1:4–7:** This is what most people understand by Dabar or Scriptures back with Mosheh, but if we look closely, the Dabar has been way before Mosheh and his commandments have been long before Sinai.
- **Jubilees 2:1–2:** We can clearly see how the angels of the presence showed the Dabar and commandments to Mosheh, explaining and declaring how everything was ordained by the Dabar of Yahuah.
- **Enoch 1:1-2:** Here we can see how Yahuah gave all the commandments and laws to Chanok (Enoc) way long before Sinai and if we read carefully, Yahuah gave him the vision of the present past and future to come.

By reading these verses in contexts and combining them we can clearly determine that all commandments were given by Yahuah and that **Dabar Yahuah** is the origine of all things and the very specific word by which everything was created.

KEY TERMS AND DEFINITIONS (WEEK 1 FOCUS)

- **Dabar** (דָּבָר): The authoritative Word, command, decree, or instruction issued by Yahuah. In this Institute, Dabar refers to the expressed will of Yahuah through which creation was spoken, commandments were given, and truth is established.
- **Dabar Yahuah:** The totality of Yahuah's authoritative instruction, including His commandments, decrees, testimonies, and revelations. **Dabar Yahuah** originates with Yahuah alone and stands as the supreme authority over humanity, Yada Yahuah (theology), and doctrine.

- **Scriptures:** The inspired written record of **Dabar Yahuah** transmitted to humanity through appointed means. In Institute usage, Scriptures are not merely religious texts, but documented divine instruction bound by covenantal authority.

- **Canon:** A term used to describe the recognized boundary of authoritative instruction. In this course, canon is evaluated according to divine origin and covenantal preservation, not human councils or traditions.

- **Tanakh (Old Testament):** The body of inspired writings documenting creation, covenant, instruction, and prophetic testimony prior to the renewed covenant era. In Institute context, these writings form a foundational portion of Dabar Yahuah.

- **New Testament:** The body of inspired writings documenting the life, teachings, death, resurrection, and covenantal fulfillment through Yahusha ha Mashiyach and His emissaries. In Institute context, these writings do not replace the Tôrâh but testify to its fulfillment.

- **Apokryfos:** A designation meaning "hidden away," used for ancient writings that were preserved yet later excluded or marginalized by religious systems. In this Institute, Apokryfos writings are evaluated by content, consistency with Dabar, and covenantal themes, not by later tradition and these writings do not replace the Tôrâh but testify to its fulfillment.

- **Angels of the Presence:** Heavenly beings associated with standing before Yahuah and involved in the transmission, witnessing, or declaration of divine instruction according to Scriptural testimony.

COVENANTAL STUDY TASK

Pause your reading and complete the following before proceeding. Engage the Scriptural text directly. Do not summarize secondary opinions.

- ***Identify where commands are given***
- ***Note how Scripture describes its origin***

FINAL THOUGHTS ON WEEK 1

"understanding that Dabar is the origin of everything and that Dabar Yahuah is his word, it will open our hearts and mind to the true meaning of Dabar Yahuah."

QUOTE REFLECTION (WEEK 1)

"Where Dabar begins, confusion ends—because the Word, of Yahuah is the beginning of all truth."

TERM I – MONTH 1- WEEK 2 — HEAVENLY TABLETS
WEEK 2 LEARNING OUTCOMES — HEAVENLY TABLETS

BY THE END OF WEEK 2, STUDENTS SHOULD BE ABLE TO:

- Explain the concept of Heavenly Tablets using Scriptural references
- Distinguish heavenly preservation from earthly transmission
- Identify Scriptural evidence for angelic witness and custody
- Explain why earthly instruction is considered a copy, not an original

INTRODUCTION TO WEEK 2

We normally trace the origin of **Dabar Yahuah** back to Mosheh and fail to understand that Dabar Yahuah, or the Word of Yahuah, is beyond humanity; that it existed since the very foundation of the world; and, more importantly, that everything is recorded and preserved in heaven. Whatever humanity has received on earth is only a fragment or a copy of the original version.

TERM I - MONTH 1 - WEEK 2 - READINGS

Chapter 1 from *Yahuah: Restoration Guide*
Watch the given videos for supplemental tools and support.

ALIGNMENT FOCUS — CHAPTER 1 (HEAVENLY RECORD EMPHASIS)

While Week 1 established that Dabar originates at Creation, Week 2 advances the discussion by identifying where that Dabar is preserved.

CHAPTER 1 READING SCOPE — WHAT TO EXTRACT

From Chapter 1 from Yahuah: Restoration Guide, extract the following distinct emphasis for Week 2:

- **Creation as a Recorded Event**

Creation is not only spoken by Dabar but ordered, measured, and recorded, revealing that divine instruction is structured and preserved beyond the physical realm.

- **Shabbath as a Heavenly Ordinance**

The Shabbath is presented as a sign kept in heaven and on earth, indicating a heavenly record governing earthly observance.

- **Angelic Witness and Custody**

Angels of the Presence and angels of sanctification appear in Creation narratives as participants and witnesses, implying the existence of a preserved heavenly testimony.

- **Earth as a Reflection, Not the Source**

What humanity experiences in Creation is shown to be a reflection of heavenly order, reinforcing the concept that earthly instruction mirrors a higher, preserved original.

Your objective in Chapter 1 for Week 2 is not to re-prove origin, but to recognize preservation:

Dabar does not merely begin with Yahuah—it remains with Yahuah, recorded and guarded in heaven.

TERM I - MONTH 1 - WEEK 2 - READINGS 2:

- **Shemoth 24:12:** Yahuah Himself writes the commandments given to Mosheh.
- **Exodus 25:9, 40:** Yahuah reveals the heavenly pattern so a copy may be made on earth.
- **Shemoth 31:18:** The tablets are written by the finger of Yahuah.
- **Jubilees 6:17–19:** Direct reference to the Heavenly Tablets as the original record.
- **Chănôk (Enoch) 81:1:** Chanok is shown the Heavenly Tablets written by Yahuah.
- **Psalm 119:89:** Dabar Yahuah is established in heaven, not on earth.

KEY TERMS AND DEFINITIONS (WEEK 2 FOCUS)

- Heavenly Tablets: The heavenly record in which Yahuah's decrees, appointed times, and judgments are established and preserved. In this Institute, Heavenly Tablets represent the original and incorruptible source of divine instruction.
- Author of the Heavenly Tablets: Yahuah Himself. The authority and permanence of the Heavenly Tablets rest solely on His authorship, not on human transmission.
- Earthly Tablets: The physical manifestation or copy of divine instruction delivered to humanity. Earthly Tablets serve as a faithful transmission of what is first established in heaven.
- Author of the Earthly Tablets: Yahuah in origin, though delivered through appointed servants. While humans may transmit the tablets, authorship remains divine.

COVENANTAL STUDY TASK

Pause your reading and complete the following before proceeding. Engage the Scriptural text directly. Do not summarize secondary opinions.

• Identify where Dabar Yahuah is recorded and preserved
• Note who writes and authors the instruction
• Observe the relationship between heavenly pattern and earthly copy

FINAL THOUGHT ON WEEK 2

"If we understand that Dabar Yahuah is the original version, written in heaven by Yahuah Himself, kept and preserved pure in heaven, then we will understand that no matter how humanity tries to delude the truth of Yahuah, it will never prosper—because His truth is already written and preserved in heaven, where no human hands can reach it."

QUOTE REFLECTION (WEEK 2)

"The earth may distort what it touches, but heaven preserves what Yahuah establishes."

TERM I – MONTH 1 – WEEK 3 — CANON VS. TRADITION
WEEK 3 LEARNING OUTCOMES — CANON VS. TRADITION

BY THE END OF WEEK 3, STUDENTS SHOULD BE ABLE TO:
- Define Tôrâh as divine instruction distinct from human canon classification
- Identify tradition as a competing authority structure
- Demonstrate how Scripture defines sin independently of culture or institution
- Evaluate doctrinal claims against Scriptural authority

INTRODUCTION TO WEEK 3
This is the eternal battle of humanity, which fail to comprehend the truth of Dabar Yahuah, because it is tamed, indoctrinated and shaped by human tradition, which at the end only leads to perdition.

What is canon: it is the Greek word used to describe the group of books or teachings accepted by traditional views, thus rejecting all the other books including those inspired (apokryfos) that do not fit into their patter. Therefore, the word canon literally means rule.

However if we look back to the original language the correct word would not be the Greek word κανών, but the Hebrew word tôrâh (⬚⬚⬚⬚), which literally means a precept or statute, especially the Decalogue or Pentateuch, law.

TERM I - MONTH 1 - WEEK 3 — READING:
Chapter 2 Reading Scope — What to Extract
While reading Chapter 2 from Yahuah: Restoration Guide, students are to focus exclusively on how divine instruction is contrasted with human authority.

EXTRACT FROM CHAPTER 2:
The definition of sin as disobedience to Tôrâh, not as cultural failure or moral sentiment.
- The presentation of Tôrâh as the sole measure of obedience, independent of

religious institutions or later classifications.

- The discussion of the Ten Commandments and the Shabbath as examples of how divine instruction is selectively reinterpreted or replaced by human tradition.
- The historical reasoning used to justify the replacement of commandment with tradition, particularly in matters of worship and observance.

Do not focus on:

- Narrative details of Yôsêph beyond their function as an example of human decision-making.
- Devotional or moral applications unrelated to authority, canon, or tradition.
- The broader historical development of Yâshâral slavery except where it illustrates consequences of disobedience.
- Comparative Yada Yahuah (theology) or denominational debates not directly tied to the question of authority.

The purpose of Chapter 2 in Week 3 is to identify how human tradition functions as a competing authority to Tôrâh, not to exhaustively study sin, slavery, or the commandments.

TERM I – MONTH 1 – WEEK 3 – READINGS 2:

- **Debarim 4:2:** Yahuah Elohiym gives specific instructions to follow his torah and not to add nor diminish, but he is talking about his torah, the real canon, not the one made up by men.
- **Matthew 15:3–9:** Yahusha reinstate the commandments given to Mosheh, the real canon, the torah of Yahuah.
- **Mark 7:6–13:** The doctrines of men versus the real torah, Yahusha himself is showing us the reality and what the truth torah is and what it is not. No traditions, no doctrines of men and Yahusha himself tells you that those who follow this traditional canon make Dabar Yahuah of no effect.
- **Enoch 8:1–3:** The torah of Yahuah is in heaven and human have received just a copy of it.

Key Terms and Definitions (Week 3 Focus)

- **Indoctrination:** The process by which belief is shaped and controlled by human systems rather than by direct engagement with Dabar Yahuah. Indoctrination replaces discernment with conformity.

- **Human Tradition:** Practices, interpretations, or teachings developed by men and elevated to authority alongside or above divine instruction. In this Institute, human tradition is evaluated strictly against Dabar Yahuah.

- **κανών (Canon):** A Greek term meaning "rule" or "measure," historically used to define accepted writings. In this module, κανών is examined critically as a human classification system, not the origin of divine authority.

- **Tôrâh (תּוֹרָה):** Instruction, law, or teaching issued by Yahuah. Tôrâh represents the true rule and measure of divine authority, existing prior to and beyond later human categorizations.

- **Decalogue:** The ten foundational commandments delivered in covenant context, representing a central expression of Yahuah's moral and covenantal instruction.

- **Pentateuch:** The first five books traditionally attributed to Mosheh, containing creation accounts, covenant formation, instruction, and legal foundations. In Institute usage, the Pentateuch is part of a broader continuum of Tôrâh, not its origin.

- **Doctrines of Men:** Teachings created or reshaped by human authority that replace, reinterpret, or nullify the commandments of Yahuah. Yahusha explicitly condemns such doctrines when they override divine instruction.

Covenantal Study Task

Pause your reading and complete the following before proceeding. Engage the Scriptural text directly. Do not summarize secondary opinions.
- *Compare Scripture vs. human tradition*

FINAL THOUGHTS ON WEEK 3

"We understand and read perfectly the real torah, the one given by Yahuah, given to us since the very beginning, given to Chanok, Abraham and finally in a more written form to Mosheh in mount Sinai. Then Yahusha himself as Yahuah, presented the real meaning and after his resurrection the writings of his followers became part of the torah, which at the end, do not say anything new, do not add, nor dimmish, only present the torah in a context where we can understand it, but never changed."

QUOTE REFLECTION (WEEK 3)

"Tradition can be inherited without truth—but Tôrâh must be received from Yahuah."

TERM I – MONTH 1 - WEEK 4 — CANONICAL GUARDIANS
WEEK 4 LEARNING OUTCOMES — CANONICAL GUARDIANS

BY THE END OF WEEK 4, STUDENTS SHOULD BE ABLE TO:
- Trace Scriptural guardianship of Tôrâh through covenantal appointment
- Identify priestly responsibility for preservation and transmission
- Distinguish covenantal authority from imperial or institutional authority
- Explain the role of Yahusha within the Malkîy-Tsedeq priesthood framework

INTRODUCTION TO WEEK 4

Custodianship of Dabar Yahuah and the Preservation of the Canon
Understanding who was entrusted with the guardianship of Dabar Yahuah is essential for understanding what constitutes the true canon of the inspired Scriptures of Yahuah. Within the Institute's restoration framework, the evidence indicates that custodianship of the Scriptures was covenantal, hereditary, and divinely assigned rather than institutional or political.

According to the Torah itself, the responsibility to guard, teach, and preserve Dabar Yahuah was not given to empires, philosophical schools, or religious institutions, but to a specific covenantal order. The priesthood of Aharon (Aaron) was divinely established and ordained as the authorized guardian of the Torah. This custodianship was exercised within the Temple order of Yahuah and was not transferable to external political or religious authorities.

The tribe of Levi (Lewiy), and more specifically the sons of Aharon, were charged with preserving, transmitting, and teaching the Torah. Within this lineage, the high priesthood of Zadok (Tsadoq) represents the faithful continuation of this custodial responsibility. Authority to preserve Dabar Yahuah remained covenantal and hereditary, rooted in obedience and priestly succession rather than institutional power or theological innovation.

Within this restoration framework, the lineage of Aharon is understood to have maintained this guardianship through priestly communities associated with locations such as Qumran and Bethabara. These custodians are distinguished from the Essenes, who inhabited nearby regions such as Ein Gedi, and whose philosophical and communal identity differed from the Temple-centered priestly lineage. From this Levitical priesthood emerged figures such as Yochanan (John) the Immerser, whose priestly origin reflects continuity with the custodians of the Torah. It is within this same covenantal context that some early followers of Yahusha are understood to have been connected to priestly lines responsible for preserving the authentic corpus of Dabar Yahuah.

By contrast, the true canon of Scripture was not preserved nor established by Constantine, the Roman Empire, nor later religious institutions. These entities did not possess covenantal authority to guard nor define the Scriptures. Through political and theological intervention, they altered, restricted, and suppressed recognized biblical writings in order to advance doctrinal paradigms that departed from revealed truth. As a result, foundational Torah-related texts—such as Jubilees and Enoch—were marginalized or removed from common use, despite their preservation within earlier priestly custodial traditions.

TERM I – MONTH 1 – WEEK 4 — CANONICAL GUARDIANS
Read Chapter 2 from Yahuah: Restoration Guide.
Watch the given videos for supplement tools and support.

Chapter 2 Reading Scope — What to Extract
While reading Chapter 2 from Yahuah: Restoration Guide, students are to focus on custody, transmission, and guardianship of Tôrâh, not on polemics against tradition.

EXTRACT FROM CHAPTER 2:
- The principle that Tôrâh predates Sinai and operates through covenantal continuity.
- The idea that divine instruction is preserved through entrusted guardianship,

not merely through written preservation.

- The distinction between authority derived from obedience and appointment versus authority derived from institution or power.
- The relationship between commandment, priestly responsibility, and faithful transmission without alteration.

Do not focus on:
- Arguments concerning Sunday vs. Shabbath as a controversy.
- Polemical critique of religious institutions beyond the issue of guardianship.
- Repetition of canon-versus-tradition arguments already addressed in

Week 3.
Personal or devotional interpretations of obedience.
The purpose of Chapter 2 in Week 4 is to identify who guards Tôrâh and how that guardianship is exercised, not to debate tradition or redefine canon.

TERM I – MONTH 1 – WEEK 4 – READINGS 2:

Bereshith 18:19: Abraham commanded his sons to keep the Torah (not the Mosaic Torah).
Bereshith 26:5: Abraham keeps the Torah of Yahuah
Shemoth 28:1: Aharon is entrusted in keeping and guarding the Torah of Yahuah
Ezekiel 44:15: The sons of Lewiy, the sons of Tsadoq presented as the real keeper and guardian of the Torah.
Psalm **110:4:** Malkîy-Tsedeq the high priest forever and the final keeper, giver and guardian of the torah (Yahusha ha Mashiyach).

KEY TERMS AND DEFINITIONS (WEEK 4 FOCUS)
- **Custodian:** A person or group entrusted with the responsibility to keep, protect, preserve, and faithfully transmit something of value. In this module, a custodian refers to those appointed to steward Dabar Yahuah without

alteration, addition, or corruption.

- **Guardian:** One who actively defends and safeguards what has been entrusted. A guardian not only preserves Scripture but also protects it from distortion, ensuring that Dabar Yahuah remains intact in teaching, transmission, and practice.

- **Priesthood:** The covenant-appointed order set apart to minister before Yahuah and to teach, preserve, and administer His Tôrâh among the people. Priesthood is not merely religious leadership; it is an authorized covenant office with defined responsibilities and boundaries.

- **High Priest:** The chief priest within the priestly order, bearing the highest covenantal responsibility for intercession, sacred service oversight, and guardianship of holy instruction. In this module, the High Priest represents authorized spiritual governance tied directly to the preservation of Dabar Yahuah.

- **Qumran:** A region near the Dead Sea associated with the preservation and copying of ancient sacred manuscripts, including those known today as the Dead Sea Scrolls. In Institute context, Qumran is referenced as a historical location connected to Scriptural preservation and priestly transmission, not as a doctrinal authority in itself.

- **Bethabara:** A geographic designation associated with the Jordan region, traditionally identified as a place of crossing and renewal. In this module, Bethabara is referenced in relation to covenantal transition, priestly activity, and preparation for restoration within the broader biblical narrative and Qumran.

- **Yahusha:** The restored Name used by the Institute for the Messiah. Yahusha ha Mashiyach is recognized as the fulfillment and perfect embodiment of Yahuah's Tôrâh, and the ultimate authority who restores proper understanding of Dabar Yahuah. In this module, Yahusha is presented as the final and faithful High Priest in covenantal fulfillment.

- **Constantine:** A Roman emperor historically associated with the formal integration of Christianity into the Roman imperial system. In this module,

Constantine is referenced as a representative of imperial religious authority, not as a covenant-appointed guardian of Scripture.

- **Roman Empire:** The political and imperial system that ruled much of the Mediterranean world during and after the Second Temple period. In this module, the Roman Empire represents state-controlled religious influence, which stands in contrast to covenant-based Scriptural guardianship established by Yahuah.

- **Book of Jubilees:** An ancient Hebrew work closely aligned with Genesis and Exodus, emphasizing covenant order, commandments, appointed times, and heavenly record. In this module, Jubilees is used to support the concepts of heavenly testimony, continuity of Tôrâh, and preservation beyond human institutions.

- **Book of Enoch:** A collection of ancient writings attributed to Chanok (Enoch), addressing heavenly revelation, judgment, rebellion, and divine instruction. In this module, Enoch is used to examine pre-Sinai instruction, heavenly record, and the conflict between truth and corruption.

- **Mosaic Torah:** The formal administration of Tôrâh delivered through Mosheh to Yâshâral. In this module, Mosaic Torah is understood as a codified transmission of instruction that already existed, not the origin of divine law.

- **Malkîy-Tsedeq:** A priest-king figure presented in Scripture as representing a priesthood order not based on Levitical descent. In this module, Malkîy-Tsedeq introduces the concept of a higher, enduring priesthood, culminating in Yahusha ha Mashiyach as the ultimate covenantal High Priest.

COVENANTAL STUDY TASK

Pause your reading and complete the following before proceeding. Engage the Scriptural text directly. Do not summarize secondary opinions.
• *Trace who was authorized to guard Scripture*

FINAL THOUGHTS ON WEEK 4

"The canon known today was not the real canon established by Yahuah and kept by the sons of Aharon, the canon known today was established and selected by false priesthood and the empire of Rome. The real torah was kept by the sons of Tsâdôq, sons of Aharon and preserved in Qumran where the Dead Sea scrolls have been found those giving us the real list of the books kept as torah."

QUOTE REFLECTION (WEEK 4)

"Yahuah preserves His truth through covenantal guardians, not through imperial power."

DEMONSTRATION OF MASTERY

STUDENTS ARE EXPECTED TO DEMONSTRATE MASTERY OF MONTH 1 CONTENT THROUGH:

- Accurate identification of Scriptural authority structures
- Clear differentiation between divine origin and human transmission
- Logical use of Scripture to support conclusions
- Faithful engagement with assigned texts without reliance on secondary theological systems

Progression to subsequent modules assumes fluency in the Core Reinforcement principles.

TERM I – MONTH 1 - CORE REINFORCEMENT GUIDE (WEEKS 1-4)

This section identifies the non-negotiable concepts established during the first month. Students are expected to be fluent in these principles before advancing.

DABAR YAHUAH IS PRE-HUMAN AND PRE-TEXTUAL (WEEK 1)

- Dabar Yahuah does not originate with Mosheh, Sinai, or written scripture.
- Divine instruction exists prior to humanity, prior to language, and prior to textual transmission.
- Written texts on earth represent manifestation, not origin.
- Any Yada Yahuah (theology) that treats the Bible as the origin of Yahuah's Word misunderstands Dabar, which is first Yahuah's living action in the world and only later becomes written witness.

If this is unclear:
Re-establish the distinction between origin and transmission.

Heavenly Preservation Precedes Earthly Reception (Week 2)

- Divine instruction is recorded, preserved, and guarded in heaven.
- Earthly tablets, writings, and covenants are copies, not originals.
- Creation itself is structured, ordered, and recorded.
- The Shabbath functions as a heavenly ordinance with earthly reflection.
- Angelic participation indicates custodianship and testimony, not symbolism.

If this is unclear:

Re-focus on preservation, not authorship or inspiration debates.

Tôrâh Is the True Measure; Canon Is a Human Construct (Week 3)

- "Canon" (κανών) is a Greek classification tool meaning "rule" or "measure."
- Tôrâh (תּוֹרָה) is divine instruction and precedes all later classifications.
- Sin is defined as disobedience to Tôrâh, not moral sentiment or cultural failure.
- Human tradition functions as a competing authority when it:
    - Adds to instruction
    - Removes commandments
    - Reinterprets obedience for convenience
- Yahusha does not abolish Tôrâh; He restores its meaning and authority.

If this is unclear:

Re-establish authority hierarchy:

Yahuah → Tôrâh → obedience

not

institution → canon → interpretation.

Tôrâh Is Guarded Through Appointment, Not Institution (Week 4)

- Tôrâh is preserved through entrusted guardianship, not institutional canonization.

- Abraham obeys Tôrâh before Sinai.
- Priestly custody (Aharon, Lewiy, Tsadoq) is based on appointment and faithfulness, not power.
- Guardianship involves:
  - Preservation without alteration
  - Transmission without innovation
  - Obedience without negotiation
- Ultimate guardianship culminates in Malkîy-Tsedeq and Yahusha as eternal mediator.

If this is unclear:

Re-focus on who guards instruction and by what authority.

Structural Principles That Govern the Entire Course

Students must also retain the following methodological foundations:

- Divine instruction flows heaven → earth, never the reverse.
- Textual authority does not equal textual origin.
- Obedience is covenantal, not institutional.
- Tradition must always be evaluated against Tôrâh, never the opposite.

Month 1 Outcome Expectation

By the end of Month 1, students should be able to:

- Distinguish origin, preservation, transmission, authority, and guardianship as separate concepts.
- Identify where human systems replace divine instruction.
- Read advanced Yada Yahuah (theological) material with controlled scope, not devotional drift.
- Articulate why Tôrâh cannot be reduced to canon, culture, or institution.

TERM I — MONTH 1 ESSAY (STRUCTURE & METHOD TRAINING)

Purpose of This Assignment

This first-month essay is not designed to test originality, but to train students in the structure, method, and authority framework required for all future MBRS essays.

Students are expected to study the provided sample essay carefully, learn its structure, logic, and Scriptural reasoning, and demonstrate understanding by responding to the prompt using the same organizational framework.

From Month 2 onward, students will apply this structure independently to new topics.

Essay Length

1,000–1,500 words

Essay Prompt

Explain how Scripture presents itself as divinely originated, canonically bounded, and authoritatively preserved from Creation onward. Support your explanation using the assigned readings.

Instructions (Important)

- This essay must follow the structure demonstrated in the Month 1 sample essay.
- Students should not invent a new format or organizational flow.
- The goal is to demonstrate:
    - understanding of authority order,
    - correct use of Scripture as evidence,
    - and ability to reason directly from Dabar Yahuah.

Required Structural Sections

Your essay must include the following sections in this order:
- Chosen Focus (Aligned with Term Content): Explain why the topic of

Scriptural authority, origin, and preservation is foundational to biblical restoration.

- Identification of the Problem and Its Ramifications: Identify how misunderstanding Scriptural authority leads to confusion, instability, or doctrinal dependence.
- False Views and Doctrines of Men: Identify common false assumptions or traditions that misrepresent the origin, authority, or boundaries of Scripture.
- Correct Scriptural Perspective (With Evidence): Use the assigned readings and Dabar Yahuah Scriptures to demonstrate:
  - divine origin of Dabar,
  - heavenly establishment,
  - canonical boundaries,
  - covenantal preservation.
- Personal Conclusion and Application: Explain how restoring correct authority helps the student and the community walk in clarity and obedience.

Source Requirements

- All Scriptural citations must come from Dabar Yahuah Scriptures.
- Hebrew and Greek term consultation should use the Dabar Yahuah Scriptures App where relevant.
- Secondary opinions, commentaries, or external theological frameworks are not permitted.

Evaluation Focus

Essays will be evaluated on:

- faithfulness to the provided structure,
- clarity of authority reasoning,
- proper use of Scripture as evidence,
- and alignment with the MBRS framework.

Instructional Note to the Student

This essay establishes the foundation for all future academic work in MBRS. Master the structure now, and you will use it throughout the program. Submission:

You will submit your essay in writing and will give your presentation of your essay in a video format, thus demonstrating your master of this month teachings and learnings. No plagiarism, no copy content, no false content, only original and truthful content will be accepted. Your master level of the concept is the key point for determining if you are ready for the next term or not.

These are some of the criteria for your evaluation:

Cite Scripture accurately, avoid speculation, demonstrate Covenantal Reasoning, show progression from Week 1 to Week 4.

SAMPLE ESSAY (MODEL FOR ALL TERMS)

When Tradition Replaces Dabar

How Students Lose Scriptural Authority and How Restoration Returns Clarity

Student Name: _____

Student ID: _____

Date (day, month, year): _____

Course: Term 1 — Month 1 (Module 1)

Word Count Target: 1,000–1,500 words

1. Chosen Topic (Aligned With This Term)

This essay addresses the problem of human tradition replacing Dabar Yahuah as the standard of truth. Term 1 establishes that Dabar originates with Yahuah from the beginning, is recorded in heavenly testimony, and is preserved through covenantal guardianship. Therefore, the conflict between tradition and Dabar is not a secondary concern; it is the central issue that determines whether

Scripture is approached as divine instruction or reduced to a human religious system.

This topic is chosen because a student cannot advance in biblical restoration without first understanding where authority comes from. When authority is misunderstood, every other category becomes confused: covenant, obedience, canon, priesthood, salvation, and even identity. Restoration begins not with new information, but with restoring the correct authority order.

2. The Problem and Its Ramifications

The Problem

The primary problem is that many believers have been trained to treat tradition, institutional doctrine, and inherited religious frameworks as equal to—or greater than—Dabar Yahuah. Even when Scripture is read, it is often filtered through systems that determine what is acceptable, orthodox, or permitted, instead of allowing Dabar to define itself.

This creates a condition where Scripture is treated as incomplete unless explained by institutions. As a result, students become dependent on authorities outside of Dabar and lose the ability to reason directly from Scripture.

Ramifications

This authority disorder produces serious consequences:

- Scripture becomes secondary.

Students may read Scripture, but they obey tradition. When asked to explain their faith, they rely on inherited frameworks rather than Dabar itself.

Canon becomes political rather than covenantal.

Students assume the boundaries of Scripture were decided by councils or empires, rather than preserved through heavenly testimony and covenant guardianship.

- Obedience becomes selective.

Commandments are treated as optional or cultural, while doctrines of men are treated as moral absolutes.

- Students become unstable and easily deceived.

Without a single authority standard, every new teaching appears plausible. The student wanders between interpretations without covenant grounding.

- Restoration becomes difficult.

Restoration requires returning to origins. A student trained by tradition often resists restoration because restoration exposes what tradition has replaced.

The core issue is therefore not disagreement, but authority: Who defines truth—Yahuah or men?

3. False Views, Traditions, and Doctrines of Men

False frameworks often appear ancient, spiritual, and organized, yet they are false because they override Dabar Yahuah.

False View 1: "Instruction begins at Sinai."

This view assumes no divine instruction existed before Mosheh. It dismisses pre-Sinai obedience, ignores covenantal faithfulness before Sinai, and marginalizes testimony such as Enoch and Abraham.

False View 2: "Canon is defined by institutional approval."

This trains students to trust councils and empires rather than covenantal guardianship and heavenly testimony.

False View 3: "Tradition is required to interpret Scripture."

This teaches that Scripture is unclear without inherited doctrine, producing dependence instead of disciplined engagement with Dabar.

False View 4: "Traditions are harmless cultural practices."

Yahusha directly confronts traditions when they override commandment. The danger is not tradition as history, but tradition as authority.

These views produce students who quote Scripture while functioning under a different authority system.

4. Correct Biblical Perspective (Supported by Scripture)

Term 1 establishes that Dabar Yahuah defines itself as divine, authoritative, bounded, and preserved.

A. Dabar Exists From the Beginning

Bereshith 1:1–3 shows that creation itself is spoken into existence. Reality begins with Dabar.

Bereshith 2:16–17 confirms that commandment and obedience existed at humanity's beginning.

Jubilees 1:4–7 and 1 Enoch 1:1–2 further testify that instruction and prophetic witness precede Sinai.

B. Dabar Is Established in Heaven

Shemoth 24:12 and 31:18 show that instruction delivered to Mosheh originates with Yahuah.

Exodus 25:9, 40 reveals the heavenly-original / earthly-copy pattern.

Jubilees 6:17–19 and Enoch 81:1 affirm the permanence of heavenly tablets.

Psalm 119:89 declares that Dabar is settled in heaven.

C. Tradition Is Condemned When It Overrides Commandment

Debarim 4:2 establishes clear boundaries.

Matthew 15:3–9 and Mark 7:6–13 show Yahusha confronting traditions that nullify Dabar. Tradition becomes deception when it replaces obedience.

D. Dabar Was Preserved Through Covenant Guardianship

Bereshith 18:19 and 26:5 show obedience before Sinai.

Shemoth 28:1 and Ezekiel 44:15 define priestly guardianship.

Psalm 110:4 introduces the Malkîy-Tsedeq order fulfilled in Yahusha, confirming continuity and preservation.

The biblical conclusion is clear: Dabar is not created, edited, or authorized by men. It originates with Yahuah, is preserved through covenant, and stands above tradition.

5. Personal Conclusion, Solution, and Community Impact

Personal Conclusion

The crisis facing modern believers is not lack of religion, but lack of authority clarity. When tradition is treated as equal to Scripture, instability follows. When Dabar is restored as the highest authority, clarity returns.

Restoration begins by submitting to Dabar, not by accumulating information.

Practical Solutions

- Restore authority order:

Dabar first. Tradition second. Institutions last.

- Develop disciplined study:

Read Scripture sequentially and prove claims by Dabar alone.

- Reject doctrinal dependence:

Explain truth using Dabar Yahuah Scriptures, not inherited frameworks.

- Teach others the same pattern:

Help families and communities return to covenant clarity.

How This Helps Others

This approach produces students who:

- recognize deception early,
- resist manipulation,
- and teach restoration with confidence and evidence.

When authority is corrected, everything becomes clearer—salvation, covenant, obedience, identity, and purpose.

Closing Reflection

"Where Dabar is restored as the highest authority, confusion loses its power—because truth is not invented on earth; it is established in heaven by Yahuah."

This quote must be included verbatim in every essay.

(Students may reflect on this quote, but may not alter it.)

TERM I - MONTH 2
ACADEMIC ORIENTATION — TERM I · MONTH 2

Month 2 advances the study of Scripture from origin and definition to custody, authority, and continuity. Students are expected to engage Scriptural testimony concerning priesthood, preservation, and covenantal transition with analytical precision and covenantal reasoning.

This module assumes mastery of Month 1 foundations, particularly the distinction between origin, preservation, transmission, and authority. Interpretations must remain grounded in Scripture itself, evaluated through covenantal appointment rather than institutional assumption.

STUDENTS ARE EXPECTED TO:
- Trace authority structures Scripturally rather than historically alone
- Distinguish legitimacy from lineage
- Evaluate priesthood according to obedience and divine authorization
- Demonstrate covenantal continuity without collapsing it into sameness

Assertions must be supported by Scriptural reasoning. Appeals to tradition, institutional authority, or later theological systems are not treated as determinative.

MODULE 2 OVERVIEW
This module teaches how Scripture was preserved and transmitted through an authorized priestly line. You will study how Yahuah assigned guardianship of His Word and how Scripture itself identifies faithful and unfaithful priesthoods. You will learn that Scripture does not leave its preservation to chance, popular opinion, or political authority. Instead, Yahuah assigns guardianship through covenant, obedience, and faithfulness, and He removes it when priesthood

becomes corrupt.

By the end of this month, the student will understand that Scriptural authority is never institutional, but always covenantal, and that all priestly authority reaches its completion and permanence in Yahusha ha Mashiyach alone.

2. Methodological Continuity Statement

Methodological Continuity — Covenant, Authority, and Transition

Module 2 continues the restorative covenantal methodology established in Module

All material is evaluated according to the following governing principles:
Priestly Authority Is Covenantal Appointed

- Authority to teach, guard, and administer divine instruction is granted by Yahuah and may be revoked upon unfaithfulness.
- Obedience Determines Legitimacy
- Lineage, office, or institutional recognition do not guarantee authority. Scripture consistently prioritizes obedience and fidelity.
- Preservation Operates Independently of Power
- Divine instruction is preserved through covenant faithfulness, not political dominance or institutional continuity.
- Transition Does Not Mean Cancellation

Covenant transitions represent fulfillment and completion, not contradiction or abandonment.

These principles govern all weekly readings, study tasks, and assessments in Month 2.

MODULE 2 LEARNING OUTCOMES

By the end of Term I – Month 2, students should be able to:

- Identify Scriptural models of authorized priestly guardianship
- Distinguish between legitimate and illegitimate priestly authority using Scriptural criteria

- Explain how priesthood can be revoked through corruption and preserved through obedience
- Demonstrate how Scripture was preserved through non-imperial, covenant-based custodianship
- Trace priestly continuity across covenant transitions without asserting replacement
- Articulate how Yahusha fulfills priestly authority according to the order of Malkîy-Tsedeq

Mastery is demonstrated through accurate Scriptural citation, covenantal logic, and coherent integration of Torah, Prophets, and Apostolic writings.

TERM I – MONTH 2 – WEEK 5 — PRIESTLY GUARDIANSHIP
THE TRANSITION OF COVENANT AUTHORITY AND THE OBSOLESCENCE OF THE LEVITICAL PRIESTHOOD

WEEK 5 LEARNING OUTCOMES — PRIESTLY GUARDIANSHIP

By the end of Week 5, students should be able to:
- Identify who was authorized to guard and administer Tôrâh under the Sinai covenant
- Explain why the Levitical priesthood was legitimate yet time-bound
- Demonstrate from Hebrews 7–8 that priesthood transition requires covenantal transition
- Explain the characteristics of the Malkîy-Tsedeq priesthood fulfilled in Yahusha ha Mashiyach

TERM I – MONTH 2 – WEEK 5 – READING

Read Chapter 3 from Yahuah: Restoration Guide
Purpose of Week 5

To establish who was authorized by Yahuah to guard, teach, and administer His Tôrâh, and to demonstrate—by Scripture alone—that priestly authority is covenantal, conditional, and transitional.

This week establishes a foundational truth of restored Yada Yahuah (theology): the Levitical priesthood was divinely appointed for a time, but has been rendered obsolete by Yahuah Himself through the establishment of the new covenant and the eternal priesthood of Yahusha according to the order of Malkîy-Tsedeq.

TERM I – MONTH 2 – WEEK 5 – READINGS 2

- **Shemoth 28:1:** Yahuah explicitly calls Aharon and his sons to minister before Him, showing that priesthood is divinely appointed, not chosen by men.
- **Bemidbar 3:5–10:** Yahuah assigns the tribe of Lewiy to assist the priesthood, guarding sacred duties, demonstrating structured guardianship under the Sinai covenant.
- **Debarim 33:8–10:** Mosheh blesses Lewiy for teaching Yahuah's judgments and Tôrâh, confirming that instruction and preservation were central priestly functions.

These passages establish the validity of the Levitical priesthood within its covenantal context.

Doctrinal Foundation: The Change of Priesthood (Hebrews 7–8)

- Êber (Hebrews) 7:12: A change in priesthood requires a change in covenantal administration.
- Êber (Hebrews) 8:8–9: Yahuah announces a new covenant, explicitly not according to the former one.
- Êber (Hebrews) 8:13: The former covenant is declared old, obsolete, and ready to vanish away.

The verdict is clear:

the Levitical priesthood is no longer required, operative, or authoritative.

The Eternal Priesthood

Scripture presents a form of priesthood that predates the Levitical system and is not dependent on tribal lineage. This priesthood is introduced through the figure of Malkîy-Tsedeq, identified as a priest of Elyon Al, and later affirmed as eternal by prophetic declaration.

Malkîy-Tsedeq and Pre-Levitical Priesthood

Before the establishment of the Levitical priesthood through Mosheh, Scripture records Malkîy-Tsedeq as functioning in a legitimate priestly role.

Key observations:

- Malkîy-Tsedeq appears prior to Levi, demonstrating that priesthood existed before the Sinai covenant.
- He blesses Abraham, and Abraham responds by offering a tithe, indicating recognized authority rather than assumed status.
- Scripture provides no genealogical record of his priesthood, distinguishing it from lineage-based systems.

This presentation establishes a priesthood defined by divine appointment, not ancestry.

Eternal Declaration in Scripture
Psalm 110:4 declares:

"You are a priest forever according to the order of Malkîy-Tsedeq."

Fulfillment and Embodiment in Yahusha ha Mashiyach

This statement:

- Confirms the existence of a non-Levitical priestly order
- Identifies this order as eternal, not temporary or transitional
- Separates priestly authority from mortal succession

The emphasis is not on personal immortality, but on enduring covenantal function.

The Eternal Priesthood and Its Fulfillment

This eternal priesthood reaches its fulfillment in Yahusha ha Mashiyach, who embodies the Malkî-Tsedeq order. In Him, priesthood is no longer expressed through repeated ceremonial practices tied to Levitical lineage, but through a completed and faithful mediation established by divine appointment.

In Yahusha:
- Priesthood is fully aligned with obedience and covenant faithfulness
- Authority is established apart from Levitical descent
- The priestly role is completed and fulfilled, not abolished

Yahusha does not replace the Tôrah; rather, He fulfills its priestly purpose. Through His perfect faithfulness and mediation, the function of the Levitical ceremonial system—sacrifice, intercession, and atonement—is brought to completion. As a result, covenant faithfulness is no longer maintained through ritual succession, but through participation in an eternal priesthood.

The eternal priesthood:
- Exists prior to Levi
- Operates by divine appointment rather than genealogy
- Is declared eternal in Scripture
- Is fulfilled and embodied in Yahusha

This affirms continuity in covenant authority while explaining the transition from a lineage-based, ceremonial priesthood to an eternal High Priest whose faithful mediation accomplishes what the Levitical system anticipated.

TERM I – MONTH – WEEK 5 – READINGS 2

Read Chapter 3 from Yahuah: Restoration Guide.
Watch the given videos for supplement tools and support.
Chapter 3 Contextual Link — Feasts as Covenant Administration and Priestly Function

Chapter 3 provides the covenantal framework necessary to understand why priestly authority is not merely a title, but a mandated administration of Yahuah's appointed times. The biblical feasts are presented as Yahuah's own môʻêdiym—appointed convocations—therefore requiring authorized mediation, teaching, and correct procedural custody. Within this framework, the priesthood is understood as an administrative office responsible for declaring, guarding, and executing covenantal order, including sacred times, convocations, and statutes.

Chapter 3 also establishes that the feasts contain historical, prophetic, and messianic dimensions, and therefore function as a structured covenant calendar through which redemption is taught and rehearsed. This aligns directly with Week 5's purpose: authority is covenantal and transitional—what is administered (Tôrâh, statutes, appointed times) requires an authorized priesthood, and the transition to the eternal priesthood of Yahusha necessarily entails the transition of covenantal administration described in Êber (Hebrews) 7–8.

Chapter 3 Reading Scope — What to Extract / What Not to Focus
While reading Chapter 3, students are to restrict their attention to those elements that clarify covenantal administration and the authorized custody of Tôrâh.

EXTRACT FROM CHAPTER 3:
- The definition of feasts as môʻêd (appointed times) belonging to Yahuah (not human tradition), and the implication that appointed times require authorized proclamation and administration.
- The presentation of feasts as a structured covenant calendar that functions as teaching, remembrance, and regulated observance within divine order.
- The repeated insistence that biblical observances are described as statutes "forever / throughout generations," and how this language functions within

covenantal frameworks of continuity and administration.

- The use of feasts as instruments of instruction that point to the Messiah (Yahusha), establishing that covenant administration includes theological formation, not mere ritual performance.

Do not focus on:
- The full calendar calculations, Gregorian date listings, or year-specific tables (these function as reference material, not the doctrinal core of Week 5).
- Culinary, celebratory, or household practice descriptions except where they illustrate the principle of regulated observance under covenant authority.
- Extended polemical comparisons with pagan holidays; the analytical focus is covenant structure and authorized administration.

Exhaustive coverage of every feast detail; Week 5 is not a comprehensive feast practicum but an authority-and-administration unit.

The purpose of Chapter 3 in Week 5 is to identify how appointed times function as covenantal administration requiring authorized stewardship, and to place that administration within the larger transition described in Êber (Hebrews) 7–8.

This order is fulfilled and embodied in Yahusha, the eternal High Priest.

Key Terms and Definitions (Week 5)
- **Priestly Guardianship:** Covenant-appointed stewardship of Dabar Yahuah
- **Levitical Priesthood:** Temporary covenantal system under Sinai
- **Malkîy-Tsedeq Priesthood:** Eternal priesthood fulfilled in Yahusha
- **Obsolete Covenant:** A system rendered void by divine action

COVENANTAL STUDY TASK

Pause your reading and complete the following before proceeding. Engage the Scriptural text directly. Do not summarize secondary opinions.
- ***Identify who guarded Tôrâh under the former covenant***
- ***Identify why that priesthood is obsolete***
- ***Identify the characteristics of the eternal priesthood***

FINAL THOUGHTS ON WEEK 5

"The priesthood of Levi served its purpose, but it could not complete redemption. Yahuah Himself declared it obsolete and established an eternal priesthood in Yahusha."

QUOTE REFLECTION

"True authority submits to what Yahuah has eternally established."

TERM I – MONTH 2- WEEK 6 — THE SONS OF TSADOQ
FAITHFUL VS CORRUPT PRIESTHOOD

Week 6 Learning Outcomes — The Sons of Tsadoq

By the end of Week 6, students should be able to:

•Distinguish faithful priesthood from corrupt priesthood using Scriptural examples

•Explain how priestly authority can be revoked despite lineage or office

•Identify obedience as the primary marker of covenantal legitimacy

•Demonstrate how mishandling instruction leads to priestly disqualification

PURPOSE OF WEEK 6

To understand how Scripture distinguishes faithful priesthood from corrupt priesthood and how authority is preserved through obedience.

TERM I – MONTH 2 – WEEK 6- READING

- **Ezekiel 44:10–16:** Only the sons of Tsadoq are permitted to draw near to Yahuah because they remained faithful.
- **1 Samuel 2:27–35:** The house of Eli is judged and removed due to corruption.
- **Malachi 2:4–8:** Priests are rebuked for causing many to stumble through false teaching.

The Scripture proves that priesthood can be revoked.

TERM I – MONTH 2 – WEEK 6 - READING 2

Read Chapter 4 from Yahuah: Restoration Guide.

Watch the given videos for supplement tools and support.

Chapter 4 Contextual Link — Language, Instruction, and Priestly Fidelity

Chapter 4 establishes the linguistic foundation necessary for understanding how priestly authority is preserved or corrupted. Scripture consistently presents the priesthood as responsible not only for ritual function, but for accurate teaching and transmission of Yahuah's instruction. Because divine revelation was given in Hebrew, fidelity to instruction necessarily includes fidelity to language, meaning, and pronunciation.

The distinction between faithful and corrupt priesthood is therefore not limited to moral failure or ritual neglect, but extends to the handling of sacred language. Corruption emerges when instruction is altered, meanings are reshaped, or divine names and terms are modified for convenience, tradition, or accommodation. Faithful priesthood, by contrast, preserves what was entrusted—without innovation, distortion, or substitution.

Within the context of Week 6, Chapter 4 reinforces that authority is preserved through precision and obedience, not through lineage alone. Those who guard instruction must also guard the language through which that instruction is transmitted.

CHAPTER 4 READING SCOPE – WHAT TO EXTRACT / WHAT NOT TO FOCUS

While reading Chapter 4, students are to restrict attention to the role of language fidelity in preserving priestly authority.

EXTRACT FROM CHAPTER 4:

- The principle that Hebrew is the original language of divine revelation and instruction.
- The relationship between accurate transmission of language and faithful teaching.
- How alterations in pronunciation, letters, or sounds function as examples of instructional corruption rather than neutral linguistic evolution.
- The theological implication that preserving divine names and terms is part of covenant stewardship.

Do not focus on:

Memorization of the entire Hebrew alphabet.

- Linguistic debates unrelated to priestly responsibility.
- Cultural or ethnic discussions detached from covenant authority.
- General language learning goals; Week 6 is not a Hebrew language course.

The purpose of Chapter 4 in Week 6 is to demonstrate that faithful priesthood includes faithful handling of revelation, and that corruption often begins with subtle alteration of instruction rather than overt rebellion.

Key Terms and Definitions (Week 6)

- **Sons of Tsadoq:** A priestly lineage identified in Scripture as remaining faithful to Yahuah during periods of widespread priestly corruption. The Sons of Tsadoq are presented as an example of covenantal authorization maintained through obedience rather than merely inherited position.
- **Faithful Priesthood:** Priestly service that remains aligned with covenant instruction through obedience, integrity, and faithfulness to divine command. A faithful priesthood preserves authority by upholding Tôrâh, regardless of changing administrations or historical pressure.
- **Corrupt Priesthood:** Priestly authority that has been compromised and ultimately removed due to disobedience, self-interest, or violation of covenant responsibility. A corrupt priesthood may retain outward office or lineage while lacking covenantal authorization.

COVENANTAL STUDY TASK

Pause your reading and complete the following before proceeding. Engage the Scriptural text directly. Do not summarize secondary opinions.
- *Identify marks of faithful priesthood*
- *Identify causes of priestly disqualification*

FINAL THOUGHTS ON WEEK 6

"Priestly authority is preserved through obedience, not inheritance."

QUOTE REFLECTION

"Faithfulness preserves authority; corruption dissolves it."

TERM I – MONTH 2 - WEEK 7 — TEMPLE & PRESERVATION

HISTORICAL CUSTODIANSHIP AND SCRIPTURAL VERIFICATION

Week 7 Learning Outcomes — Temple & Preservation

By the end of Week 7, students should be able to:

- Identify Scriptural locations and mechanisms of preservation
- Distinguish preservation of text from visibility, usage, or institutional control
- Explain the significance of Qumran and the Dead Sea Scrolls for Scriptural verification
- Demonstrate that preservation does not equal canon formation

Read Chapter 5 from Yahuah: Restoration Guide

Purpose of Week 7

To identify where Scripture was preserved and to verify preservation historically and Scripturally.

TERM I – MONTH 2 - WEEK 7 - READING

- **Deuteronomy 31:24–26:** The Tôrâh is placed beside the Ark of the Covenant.
- **2 Kings 22:8:** The Book of the Tôrâh is rediscovered, proving survival despite neglect.
- **Nehemiah 8:1–3:** Public reading restores understanding.
- **Sirach 24:23–29:** Wisdom is identified with the Tôrâh of Mosheh.

Chapter 5 Integration — Preservation of the Name within the Preserved Text

Chapter 5 from **Yahuah: Restoration Guide** contributes to Week 7 by addressing what was preserved, not merely where it was preserved. The Scriptures assigned this week establish that the Tôrâh was deposited beside the Ark, rediscovered after periods of neglect, and restored through public reading. Chapter 5 complements this evidence by demonstrating that even when usage, pronunciation, or public acknowledgment was suppressed, the text itself remained intact.

Within the scope of Temple and preservation, Chapter 5 shows that the divine Name (יהוה) endured within the Hebrew manuscripts despite removal or substitution in later translations. This confirms the Scriptural pattern already established in Week 7: preservation does not depend on continuous institutional faithfulness, public practice, or imperial approval. Preservation is maintained by Yahuah Himself, even when custodians fail.

READING SCOPE FOR CHAPTER 5 (WEEK 7 CONTROL)

Students are to extract:

- Evidence that the divine Name remained embedded in the Hebrew text despite historical suppression.
- The distinction between textual preservation and liturgical or translational alteration.
- Confirmation that removal in translation does not equal loss of the original Scriptural record.
- Alignment with non-imperial custody and wilderness-style preservation patterns (consistent with Qumran).

Students are NOT to focus on:

- Devotional formulas or pronunciation practices.
- Polemical debates over religious traditions.
- Linguistic arguments unrelated to preservation.
- Expanding the chapter beyond verification of Scriptural survival.

For Week 7, Chapter 5 is read solely as evidence that preservation includes the integrity of the text itself, reinforcing that what Yahuah establishes cannot be erased—only ignored, until rediscovered.

Qumran and the Dead Sea Scrolls

The discovery of the **Dead Sea** Scrolls at **Qumran** (1947–1956) represents one of the most significant archaeological finds related to the Hebrew Scriptures. These manuscripts, dated approximately **250 BCE to 70 CE**, predate previously known Hebrew biblical manuscripts by nearly a thousand years and provide direct evidence of how Scripture was preserved during the Second Temple period.

Faithful Transmission

The Dead Sea Scrolls demonstrate that the Hebrew Scriptures were transmitted with remarkable accuracy over long periods of time.

Evidence:

- Biblical texts found at Qumran (including Isaiah, Psalms, Deuteronomy, and others) closely align with later Masoretic manuscripts.
- The **Great Isaiah Scroll (1QIsaᵃ)**, dated to around the 2nd century BCE, shows **substantial agreement in wording, structure, and meaning** with medieval Hebrew texts.
- Variations that do exist are primarily:
  o spelling differences
  o word order
  o minor grammatical forms
     These do **not alter doctrinal meaning.**

This level of consistency demonstrates that Scripture was not freely rewritten or corrupted but was transmitted with intentional care and fidelity, confirming continuity rather than reinvention.

Priestly Preservation

The Scrolls reveal that Scriptural custody was maintained by communities deeply concerned with ritual purity, covenant faithfulness, and obedience to Tôrâh.

Evidence:

- Many Qumran texts emphasize:
    - priestly authority
    - purity laws
    - appointed times
    - covenant obedience

- The community behind the Scrolls is widely understood to have included priestly and Levitical leadership, devoted to guarding sacred texts.
- Scribal practices show:
    - disciplined copying methods
    - oreverence for the divine Name
    - structured transmission rather than casual reproduction

Scripture was preserved by covenant-oriented guardians, not political administrators or imperial institutions. The priestly character of the manuscripts reflects continuity with biblical models of custodianship.

Non-Imperial Custody

The Dead Sea Scrolls provide clear evidence that Scriptural preservation occurred **outside of imperial control.**

Evidence:

- The Scrolls were copied and stored in:
    - caves
    - desert settlements
    - isolated religious communities
    —not in Roman archives or state-sponsored religious centers.
- Several texts explicitly critique:

- corrupt priesthoods
- centralized authority
- compromised leadership in Jerusalem
- The manuscripts predate the later Roman-aligned Christian institutional system, demonstrating that Scripture existed and was guarded independently of imperial endorsement.

The preservation of Scripture was carried out by covenant-faithful communities rather than by empires. This challenges later claims that imperial systems were the primary guardians of biblical truth.

The Dead Sea Scrolls confirm that:
- **Faithful transmission** preserved Scriptural content with remarkable accuracy.
- **Priestly preservation** maintained Scripture within covenant-based communities.
- **Non-imperial custody** ensured that divine instruction was guarded apart from political power.

Together, these findings affirm that Scripture was sustained through obedience, discipline, and covenant responsibility, not through empire or institutional authority. They witness preservation but do not define canon.

Yochanan and Priesthood

Luke 1 confirms Yochanan's priestly lineage.

His wilderness ministry aligns with covenant restoration and preparation for Yahusha.

Temples: Then and Now

Throughout Scripture, the concept of the temple reflects how Yahuah dwells among His people and how His instruction is preserved. While the form of the temple changes over time, its covenantal purpose remains consistent. The transition from a physical structure to a living, embodied dwelling does not represent contradiction, but progression within covenant order.

Then: Physical and Custodial

In the earlier covenantal administrations, the temple was a physical location appointed by Yahuah for sacred service, teaching, and preservation.

Key Characteristics:

- A defined, consecrated structure (Tabernacle and later the Temple in Yarushalayim)
- Guarded by priests and Levites, whose responsibilities included:
  - teaching Tôrâh
  - preserving sacred writings
  - maintaining ritual purity

Functioned as a custodial center, ensuring that covenant instruction was protected and transmitted faithfully

Purpose:

The physical temple served as:

- a visible sign of Yahuah's dwelling among His people
- an ordered system for safeguarding covenant knowledge

The presence of a building did not limit Yahuah; rather, it provided structure and accountability within the covenant community.

Now: Covenantal and Embodied

With the fulfillment of the covenant through the Messiah, the locus of dwelling and preservation shifts from stone to people.

Key Characteristics:

- The covenant community itself becomes the dwelling place
- Instruction is internalized rather than stored in a single location
- Faithful preservation is carried out through:

- obedience
- teaching
- lived embodiment of Tôrâh

This transition emphasizes:
- relational faithfulness over geographic centralization
- continuity of instruction rather than abandonment of order

No Contradiction, Only Continuity

The movement from a location-based temple to a Spirit-indwelt people represents a change in form, not authority or content.
- **Then:** covenant preserved through physical custodianship
- **Now:** covenant preserved through faithful embodiment

Both operate under the same divine instruction and purpose.

Summary Statement:

Preservation did not shift away from covenant order, but deeper into it. What was once guarded in sacred space is now carried within a faithful people, ensuring continuity rather than disruption.

Key Terms and Definitions (Week 7)

- **Temple:** A covenantal appointed dwelling place where Yahuah's presence, instruction, and order were stewarded through priestly service. The Temple functioned as a center for teaching, preservation of sacred testimony, and regulated covenant life, rather than merely a physical structure.
- **Ark of the Covenant:** A sacred vessel designated to house the tablets of testimony, representing the authoritative witness of Yahuah's covenant. The Ark served as a focal point of divine presence, covenant accountability, and remembrance within Yâshâral's worship and instruction.
- **Public Reading:** The communal proclamation of covenant instruction before the people, intended to restore understanding, renew obedience, and re-establish alignment with Yahuah's commands. Public reading functioned as both teaching and corrective restoration within the covenant community.

COVENANTAL STUDY TASK

Pause your reading and complete the following before proceeding. Engage the Scriptural text directly. Do not summarize secondary opinions.

- *Identify preservation locations*
- *Identify restoration mechanisms*

FINAL THOUGHTS ON WEEK 7

"Scripture survives neglect because Yahuah preserves it."

QUOTE REFLECTION

"When the Word is rediscovered, restoration begins."

TERM I – MONTH 2 – WEEK 8 — PRIESTLY CONTINUITY
FROM LINEAGE TO ETERNAL FULFILLMENT
Week 8 Learning Outcomes — Priestly Continuity

By the end of Week 8, students should be able to:
- Trace priestly continuity from lineage-based administration to eternal fulfillment
- Distinguish fulfillment from replacement in covenant transitions
- Integrate Luke, Hebrews, and prophetic testimony into a single covenant narrative
- Explain how Yahusha completes priestly authority without abolishing Tôrâh

Read Chapter 5 from Yahuah: Restoration Guide
Purpose of Week 8
To trace priestly continuity across Testaments and establish fulfillment in Yahusha.

TERM I – MONTH 2 – WEEK 8 – READING
- **Luke 1:5–17:** The renewed covenant emerges from priestly lineage.
- **John 1:19–28:** Priestly legitimacy is questioned during transition.
- **Hebrews 7:11–17:** The eternal priesthood replaces the incomplete system.

Luke and Hebrews — One Testimony
The writings commonly known as Luke and Hebrews present a unified testimony concerning covenant continuity and fulfillment. Rather than introducing competing Yada Yahuah (theological) systems, these texts function together to document historical preparation and covenantal completion within the same divine purpose.

Luke: Historical Continuity
The account attributed to Luke carefully documents the historical setting in which covenant restoration unfolds.

Key contributions:

- Records priestly service, Temple activity, and covenant obedience in the Second Temple period
- Preserves continuity between the Hebrew Scriptures and the events surrounding the Messiah
- Presents covenant transitions as rooted in history, not as abstract theology
- Luke's narrative demonstrates that the events leading to fulfillment occur within established covenant order, not outside of it.

Hebrews: Covenantal Fulfillment

The writing known as Hebrews addresses the covenantal meaning of those historical events.

Key contributions:

- Explains the priestly significance of Yahusha's role
- Interprets transitions in priesthood as fulfillment rather than cancellation
- Affirms continuity of divine instruction while clarifying its completed priestly administration

Hebrews provides theological clarification without detaching from Scriptural foundations.

Yochanan (John): Preparation

Yochanan functions as the final preparatory voice within the existing covenant structure.

Key contributions:

- Calls for repentance and restoration, not innovation
- Operates within priestly lineage and Temple context
- Prepares the people for covenant realignment rather than replacement

His role bridges expectation and fulfillment.

Yahusha: Fulfillment

Yahusha embodies the fulfillment of covenant instruction and priestly purpose.

Key contributions:

- Completes the priestly role through perfect obedience
- Fulfills prophetic and covenantal expectations
- Establishes enduring priestly mediation without abolishing Tôrâh

In Yahusha, covenant intention reaches completion, not contradiction.

Summary

- Luke records historical continuity
- Hebrews explains covenantal fulfillment
- Yochanan prepares through restoration
- Yahusha fulfills through embodiment

Together, these testimonies present a single, coherent covenant narrative rather than divided theological perspectives.

CHAPTER 5 INTEGRATION — THE NAME AS A MARKER OF PRIESTLY CONTINUITY

Chapter 5 from Yahuah: Restoration Guide supports Week 8 by addressing continuity through identification rather than location. Whereas Week 7 focused on preservation of the text, Week 8 examines who carries covenant authority across transitions. Chapter 5 contributes by demonstrating that the divine Name functions as a continuous covenant marker across priestly administrations.

In Luke 1, priestly lineage is preserved; in John 1, priestly authority is questioned during transition; in Hebrews 7, priesthood is fulfilled eternally in Yahusha. Chapter 5 complements this trajectory by showing that while priestly roles, locations, and administrations change, the Name remains constant, linking lineage-based priesthood to eternal fulfillment. The persistence of the Name across Testaments reinforces that continuity is not broken, but transferred and completed.

READING SCOPE FOR CHAPTER 5 (WEEK 8)

Students are to extract:

- How the divine Name functions as an identifier of covenant continuity across generations.
- The role of the Name in linking priestly lineage (Luke) with priestly

fulfillment (Hebrews).

- Evidence that continuity does not require institutional sameness, but covenantal consistency.
- How Yahusha embodies fulfillment without severing what preceded Him.

Students are NOT to focus on:

- Preservation arguments already addressed in Week 7.
- Translation controversies unrelated to priestly continuity.
- Devotional or polemical application of naming practices.
- Repetition of suppression or restoration history.

For Week 8, Chapter 5 is read not as a preservation study, but as evidence that what Yahuah establishes—Name, covenant, authority—remains continuous until fulfilled in Yahusha.

Key Terms and Definitions (Week 8)

- **Priestly Continuity:** The ongoing transmission of covenantal authority and responsibility from one appointed priestly administration to another, without interruption in divine instruction or purpose. Priestly continuity affirms that Yahuah's covenant order is maintained through faithful stewardship rather than terminated by historical change.
- **Renewed Covenant:** The covenantal fulfillment in which existing divine instruction is reaffirmed, internalized, and rightly applied through the Messiah, rather than abolished or replaced. The renewed covenant emphasizes restoration of obedience and understanding, not cancellation of Tôrâh.
- **Transitions of Priesthood:** The divinely directed process by which covenantal priestly roles move from one administration to another in accordance with Yahuah's purpose, culminating in completion rather than disruption. Such transitions preserve continuity while bringing the covenant order to its intended fullness.

COVENANTAL STUDY TASK

Pause your reading and complete the following before proceeding. Engage the Scriptural text directly. Do not summarize secondary opinions.

• Trace continuity

• Identify fulfillment vs replacement

FINAL THOUGHTS ON WEEK 8

"Yahuah completes what He establishes."

QUOTE REFLECTION

"Continuity proves covenant faithfulness."

TERM I — MONTH 2 - REINFORCEMENT TO DO (WEEKS 5–8)

PURPOSE

This section exists to reinforce core Yada Yahuah (theological) foundations from Month 2.

If any of the following concepts are unclear, the student must return to the corresponding week before proceeding.

Priesthood Is Covenantal Appointed (Week 5)

The student must clearly understand that:

- Priesthood is authorized by Yahuah, not by human election.
- The Levitical priesthood was:
  - Legitimate
  - Time-bound
  - Covenant-specific
- Hebrews establishes:
  - A change of priesthood
  - A corresponding change of covenantal administration
- Yahusha functions as:
  - High Priest
  - According to Malkîy-Tsedeq
  - Eternal and non-genealogical

If the student still believes priesthood is permanent by lineage alone, Week 5 must be reviewed.

Authority Is Preserved Through Obedience, Not Office (Week 6)

The student must be able to distinguish:

- Faithful priesthood vs corrupt priesthood
- Lineage vs legitimacy

- Covenantal authorization vs disqualification

Key conclusions:
- Authority can be revoked
- Obedience preserves access
- Corruption nullifies authority
- The Sons of Tsadoq are the Scriptural model of covenant fidelity

If the student assumes religious office guarantees authority, Week 6 must be reviewed.

Preservation Does Not Depend on Visibility or Power (Week 7)

The student must grasp that:
- Scripture survives neglect, suppression, and exile
- Preservation occurred:
  - Beside the Ark
  - In the Temple
  - In the wilderness
  - Outside imperial control
- Rediscovery is a recurring Scriptural pattern
- Preservation does not equal canon formation

The student must also understand:
- Public reading restores understanding
- Loss of access does not equal loss of text

If the student equates preservation with continuous institutional control, Week 7 must be reviewed.

Continuity Is Fulfilled, Not Cancelled (Week 8)

The student must be able to trace:
- Lineage → transition → fulfillment
- Luke as historical continuity

- Hebrews as covenantal completion

Key conclusions:
- Continuity does not mean sameness
- Fulfillment does not equal abolition
- Yahusha completes what precedes Him
- Covenant authority is transferred, not erased

If the student believes the New Covenant cancels what came before, Week 8 must be reviewed.

Cumulative Month 2 Master Principle
The student should now be able to articulate the following without contradiction:
Yahuah establishes covenant structures, preserves them through obedience, allows transitions by His will, and fulfills them without breaking continuity. Failure to articulate this principle indicates insufficient mastery of Month 2.

Mandatory Student Action
- Before beginning Month 3, the student must:
- Re-read any week where confusion remains
- Reconcile Hebrews with Torah, not against it
- Distinguish preservation, authority, continuity, and fulfillment as separate but related categories

Academic Positioning Note
This module engages Scriptural texts and historical evidence through a covenantal evaluation framework. While alternative scholarly models exist regarding priesthood, canon formation, and institutional authority, this Institute assesses legitimacy according to Scriptural testimony and covenantal appointment rather than later ecclesiastical consensus.
Engagement with ancient sources such as Jubilees, Enoch, and the Dead Sea

Scrolls is conducted for their evidentiary value concerning preservation and continuity, not as appeals to later tradition.

Assessment Alignment — Month 2

Each week of Month 2 contributes directly to the cumulative essay assessment:

- **Week 5** establishes the framework of authorized priesthood
- **Week 6** defines legitimacy through obedience and faithfulness
- **Week 7** verifies preservation historically and Scripturally
- **Week 8** demonstrates continuity and fulfillment in Yahusha

Students should integrate all four dimensions—authority, obedience, preservation, and continuity—into a single coherent covenantal explanation.

MONTH 2 ESSAY

Length: 1,000–1,500 words

Prompt:

Explain how Scripture identifies its authorized guardians and how priestly faithfulness preserves canonical trust. Support your explanation using the assigned readings.

Students must follow the **LOCKED ESSAY TEMPLATE** established in Month 1.

Closing Reflection Quote (Mandatory)

"Where Dabar is restored as the highest authority, confusion loses its power—because truth is not invented on earth; it is established in heaven by Yahuah."

TERM I - MONTH 3
ACADEMIC ORIENTATION — TERM I · MONTH 3

Month 3 trains students to evaluate the Apokryfos as preserved covenant witnesses within the Institute's restored framework. Students will analyze concealment, transmission, doctrinal continuity, and covenant language unity as covenant mechanisms—not as later institutional debates.

This module is not designed to argue emotionally for or against later canons. It is designed to teach disciplined covenant reasoning: how preserved writings clarify teachings already established, how continuity functions across covenants, and how meaning is preserved under pressure.

Students are expected to:
- Engage primary texts directly and contextually
- Distinguish preservation from institutional canonization
- Demonstrate continuity through intertextual comparison
- Track doctrine through covenant definitions rather than later theological categories
- Use precise terms and controlled conclusions supported by cited passages
- Unsupported assertions are not accepted. Conclusions must be traceable to assigned readings.

MODULE 3 OVERVIEW

This module studies the Apokryfos as preserved, authoritative covenant witnesses within the restored biblical framework. The purpose of this module is not to argue against later institutional canons, but to teach students how Scripture itself preserves, transmits, and clarifies truth across generations. The Apokryfos were not written to replace the Tôrâh or the Prophets. They exist to preserve covenant knowledge, to clarify doctrines already established, and to maintain continuity between the foundations of the Tôrâh and the teachings assumed in the Renewed Covenant writings.

Students will learn that Scripture was never "silent" between testaments. Instead, specific writings were preserved under priestly guardianship, protected from misuse and distortion until their appointed time of understanding.

By the end of this month, the student will understand that the Apokryfos:

- were preserved intentionally, not accidentally
- were concealed for protection, not rejection
- do not introduce new doctrine
- clarify teachings assumed by Yahusha and the emissaries
- demonstrate doctrinal continuity across covenants
- expose the false idea of a "silent" intertestamental period

Yadaʿ Yahuah — Continuity of Knowing and Covenant Meaning

Module 3 continues the restorative covenantal methodology used in Modules 1–2 while applying it to preserved writings commonly designated as Apokryfos.

This module is governed by the following interpretive principles:

- Concealment Does Not Equal Rejection
- Scripture demonstrates that Yahuah governs revelation timing. Hidden instruction may be preserved for protection until an appointed time of understanding.
- Preservation Is Covenantal, Not Institutional
- Texts survive through covenant guardianship and divine preservation, not through empire, popularity, or centralized religious control.
- Continuity Is Demonstrated by Pattern and Meaning
- Continuity is identified through repeated covenant themes, expectations, and doctrinal definitions across writings—not through institutional labeling.
- Covenantal Bridge Method
- Apokryfos function as preserved witnesses that carry forward covenant patterns later assumed and fulfilled in Renewed Covenant writings.

- Covenant Language Safeguards Doctrine

Key covenant terms preserve doctrinal meaning across time. Language is treated as a carrier of covenant faithfulness, not a cultural accident.

These principles govern all readings, weekly tasks, and assessments in Month 3.

MODULE 3 LEARNING OUTCOMES

By the end of Term I – Month 3, students should be able to:

- Explain why concealment can be divinely governed and covenantal purposeful
- Identify how preserved writings function as covenant witnesses rather than alternative doctrine
- Demonstrate how Apokryfos function as a Covenantal Bridge between earlier covenant foundations and Renewed Covenant fulfillment
- Defend resurrection hope as a pre-existing covenant expectation rather than a late doctrinal invention
- Distinguish preservation of text and meaning from institutional canonization
- Demonstrate unity of covenant language by tracing consistent covenant terms across multiple writings
- Produce a structured argument supported by explicit textual references from assigned readings

Mastery is demonstrated through accurate citation, covenant reasoning, and coherence across texts.

TERM I - MONTH 3 - WEEK 9 —
WHY THE APOKRYFOS EXIST
HIDDEN YET PRESERVED BY DIVINE DESIGN

Week 9 Learning Outcomes — Why the Apokryfos Exist

By the end of Week 9, students should be able to:

- Distinguish concealment from rejection using Scriptural evidence
- Explain revelation as divinely timed and covenant-directed
- Identify how preservation can function as protection against distortion
- Define Apokryfos within the Institute's covenantal custodianship framework

PURPOSE OF WEEK 9

The purpose of this week is to establish a foundational principle for all restored study: concealment does not equal rejection. Many students approach the Apokryfos assuming that what is hidden must be false, dangerous, or uninspired. Scripture itself refutes this assumption.

Yahuah governs revelation. He determines what is revealed, when it is revealed, and to whom it is revealed. Preservation and concealment are often acts of divine protection, not loss or corruption.

TERM 1 – MONTH 3- WEEK 9 - READING

- **Deuteronomy 29:29:** This passage establishes that not all truth is revealed at the same time. Some matters belong to Yahuah, while others are revealed for obedience. Revelation serves covenant purpose, not curiosity.
- **Daniel 12:4, 9–10:** Daniel is commanded to seal certain words until an appointed time. This proves that concealment can be commanded by Elohiym Himself and is not the result of human failure.
- **Sirach (Prologue):** The prologue explains the careful transmission of wisdom across generations and languages, affirming preservation rather than innovation.

- **Sirach 24:30–34:** Wisdom is described as abundant and overflowing beyond a single generation, showing that knowledge may exist long before it is fully understood.

Teaching Explanation

The Apokryfos exist because some covenant knowledge required protection before revelation. These writings were preserved to prevent distortion, misuse, and premature interpretation. They were hidden for safeguarding, not suppression.

KEY TERMS AND DEFINITIONS (WEEK 9)

- **Apokryfos:** Writings preserved under covenantal guardianship that were intentionally safeguarded rather than broadly circulated. The term "hidden" refers to the method and timing of preservation, not to a lack of spiritual value or authority within covenant instruction.
- **Concealment:** The deliberate withholding of revelation by Yahuah until an appointed covenantal time, ensuring that preserved instruction is revealed according to divine purpose rather than human readiness or demand.
- **Revelation:** The divinely timed unveiling of previously preserved truth, made known in accordance with covenant purpose and fulfillment rather than through innovation or alteration.

COVENANTAL STUDY TASK

Pause your reading and complete the following before proceeding. Engage the Scriptural text directly. Do not summarize secondary opinions.

- ***Distinguish concealment from rejection***
- ***Identify divine timing in revelation and preservation***

FINAL THOUGHTS ON WEEK 9

"Hidden does not mean rejected; it means appointed for revelation."

QUOTE REFLECTION

"Yahuah conceals truth to protect it, then reveals it to restore understanding."

DOCTRINAL CLARIFICATION
WHAT WE MEAN BY "TÔRÂH" IN THIS INSTITUTE

Before proceeding further, students must understand how the word Tôrâh is used in this Institute.

Tôrâh does not simply mean "law." It means instruction, teaching, and divine direction. While the Pentateuch is foundational, Tôrâh itself is broader than five books. It includes covenant instruction, moral teaching, and preserved testimony guarded by appointed custodians.

When this Institute refers to certain writings as functioning within Tôrâh, it does not mean they add commandments or override Scripture. It means they operate within the instructional framework of covenant teaching, reinforcing and clarifying what Yahuah already established.

PRESERVED APOKRYFOS UNDER PRIESTLY CUSTODIANSHIP
Instructional Witnesses of the Covenant

The following writings were preserved by covenant guardians, including priestly custodians associated with Qumran and related traditions. They were preserved because they aligned doctrinally, supported covenant Yada Yahuah (theology), and clarified teachings already present in the Tôrâh and the Prophets.

These writings are presented for historical, instructional, and covenantal insight, demonstrating how faithful communities preserved wisdom, instruction, and identity beyond centralized institutions.

- **Chănôk (Enoch):** An ancient instructional collection associated with the early patriarchal period, emphasizing heavenly order, judgment, and pre-Sinai instruction. Enoch provides insight into covenant responsibility prior to institutional priesthood.
- **Yôbêl (Jubilees):** A retelling of Genesis and Exodus structured around appointed times, covenant order, and heavenly record. Jubilees emphasizes continuity of Tôrâh and calendar faithfulness beyond later political institutions.

- **Bên Sirâ (Sirach):** A wisdom text from the Second Temple period focused on ethical instruction, reverence for Tôrâh, and practical covenant living within daily life.
- **Chokmâh Shelômôh (Wisdom of Solomon):** A wisdom work addressing righteousness, judgment, and covenant faithfulness, written to strengthen identity and obedience among Yâshâral in a Hellenistic environment.
- **1 & 2 Ezrâ (Esdras):** Texts reflecting post-exilic struggle, restoration, and divine justice, addressing questions of covenant endurance after national judgment.
- **Ṭôbîyâhû (Tobit):** A narrative emphasizing covenant faithfulness, prayer, and obedience among Yâshâraliy living in dispersion, highlighting trust in divine providence outside the land.
- **Tephillâh Menashsheh (Prayer of Manasseh):** A penitential prayer expressing repentance and restoration, traditionally associated with exile and covenant humility before Yahuah.
- **Bârûk:** A companion work connected with Jeremiah's prophetic tradition, focusing on repentance, wisdom, and covenant hope during exile.
- **Sêpher Yirmeyâhû (Letter of Jeremiah):** A didactic letter warning against idolatry, reinforcing covenant loyalty among Yâshâraliy living under foreign rule.
- **Shôshannâh (Susanna):** A narrative highlighting justice, false testimony, and righteous judgment, reinforcing covenant ethics and accountability.
- **Tephillâh Ăzaryâhû (Prayer of Azariah):** A prayer emphasizing repentance and faithfulness during trial, reinforcing trust in Yahuah amid persecution.
- **Bêl Tannîyn (Bel and the Dragon):** A narrative exposing idolatry and deception, reinforcing covenant loyalty and discernment in foreign religious environments.

These writings were preserved because they served instruction, not innovation. They stand within the covenant continuum, not outside of it.

CHAPTER LINK — YAHUAH: RESTORATION GUIDE (CHAPTER 6)

Constantine and the Council of Nicaea

Purpose

This section is not a historical survey of Roman Christianity. Students are instructed to extract only what directly explains why concealment became necessary.

WHAT TO EXTRACT FROM CHAPTER 6

- How imperial authority, not priestly guardianship, determined religious control
- How non-Levitical, non-covenantal authorities assumed interpretive power
- How political unity required replacement theology, not preservation
- Why writings outside imperial control were marginalized, hidden, or demonized

What NOT to Focus On

- Polemics
- Emotional reactions
- Comparative religion debates
- Arguments about modern denominations

The instructional objective is to understand why Apokryphal preservation became necessary, not to debate Roman history.

Chapter 6 demonstrates that concealment was not accidental. Once covenant authority was replaced by empire, **truth preservation required separation**. Hidden texts survived because they were guarded outside imperial systems.

Matthew 24:24

"For false Mâshîyach and false prophets will arise and perform great signs and wonders, so that, if possible, they will deceive even the elect."

concealment was protection, not loss.

The Apokryfos were not rejected by Yahuah. They were **shielded from empire.** They waited for restoration.

TERM I - MONTH 3 — WEEK 10: COVENANTAL BRIDGE
THE RIGHTEOUS SUFFERER ACROSS THE WRITINGS

Week 10 Learning Outcomes — Covenantal Bridge

By the end of Week 10, students should be able to:

- Demonstrate continuity between Apokryfos and Renewed Covenant texts through intertextual alignment
- Explain the "righteous sufferer" as a preserved covenant pattern rather than a later invention
- Define Covenantal Bridge, vindication, and righteous sufferer as covenant categories
- Use comparative reading to argue continuity without asserting doctrinal innovation

PURPOSE OF WEEK 10

To demonstrate how the Apokryfos function as a Covenantal Bridge, preserving themes and expectations later fulfilled and assumed in the Renewed Covenant.

TERM I - MONTH 3 - WEEK 10 - READING

- **Wisdom of Solomon 2:12–20:** Describes the righteous one being mocked, tested, condemned, and killed because his life exposes the wicked. This passage preserves a messianic expectation before Yahusha's ministry.
- **Wisdom of Solomon 5:1–5:** Describes the vindication of the righteous after suffering, revealing the blindness of those who rejected him.
- **Matthew 27:39–43:** The mockery of Yahusha mirrors Wisdom's language precisely, demonstrating continuity rather than coincidence.
- **Acts 7:51–53:** Stephan confirms that rejection of the righteous is a historical pattern, not a new event.

The Renewed Covenant does not invent the suffering Messiah. It reveals what was already testified.

Read Chapter 7 from **Yahuah: Restoration Guide**

The First Bibles - Alignment Focus — Canonical Transmission
Chapter 7 establishes the historical transmission of Scripture from Hebrew to Greek and Latin, demonstrating that while imperial systems shaped later Bible circulation, earlier covenant testimony remained preserved.

From Chapter 7, students are to recognize:
- That early Bible circulation relied on translations rather than original Hebrew custodianship.
- That imperial and ecclesiastical authority influenced canon distribution but did not originate covenant testimony.
- That preserved writings existed prior to later canon consolidation, allowing themes such as the righteous sufferer to remain intact across generations.
- That continuity between Wisdom literature and Renewed Covenant writings is the result of preservation, not retroactive invention.

Key Terms and Definitions (Week 10)
- Covenantal Bridge: A preserved Scriptural witness that links earlier covenant expectation with later fulfillment, demonstrating continuity of divine purpose across time rather than theological rupture. A Covenantal Bridge shows how promise, pattern, and instruction are carried forward into fulfillment.
- Righteous Sufferer: A faithful covenant servant who remains obedient amid persecution, injustice, or rejection, whose suffering serves as testimony rather than disqualification and is ultimately answered by divine vindication. This pattern appears repeatedly in covenant history and points toward fulfillment.
- Vindication: The act by which Yahuah publicly and covenantal confirms the righteousness of a faithful servant after suffering, demonstrating that obedience—not opposition or suffering—determines legitimacy and authority.

COVENANTAL STUDY TASK

Pause your reading and complete the following before proceeding. Engage the Scriptural text directly. Do not summarize secondary opinions.

- ***Trace the righteous sufferer pattern across the writings***
- ***Identify continuity between preserved expectation and revealed fulfillment***

FINAL THOUGHTS ON WEEK 10

"The Renewed Covenant reveals what the Apokryfos preserved."

QUOTE REFLECTION

"What was written in silence is revealed in fulfillment."

TERM I: MONTH 3 — WEEK 11: DOCTRINAL CLARITY
RESURRECTION AND COVENANT HOPE

Week 11 Learning Outcomes — Doctrinal Clarity

By the end of Week 11, students should be able to:

- Defend resurrection doctrine as preserved covenant hope prior to the Renewed Covenant writings
- Distinguish doctrinal preservation from chronological or calendrical corruption
- Explain covenant hope as continuity under exile, judgment, and restoration
- Use assigned readings to show that Yahusha confirms established covenant doctrine

PURPOSE OF WEEK 11

To establish that resurrection doctrine did not originate in the Renewed Covenant, but was preserved, clarified, and expected long before.

TERM I - MONTH 3 - WEEK 11 - READING

Resurrection is presented in Scripture as a preserved covenant expectation, progressively affirmed rather than newly introduced.

Early Covenant Witness to Resurrection

Long before the Second Temple period, resurrection hope is already present within preserved covenant instruction.

Chănôk (Enoch) presents resurrection as a settled expectation:

- The righteous are preserved for restoration and vindication
- Judgment and renewal occur after death
- Faithful obedience is not rendered meaningless by mortality

Yôbêl (Jubilees) reinforces this hope by:

- Linking covenant faithfulness with restoration beyond death
- Emphasizing divine remembrance and future renewal

- Presenting resurrection within covenant order, not speculative theology

These texts demonstrate that resurrection hope existed within covenant teaching, not as a later innovation.

Exilic and Post-Exilic Affirmation

Baruch 3:9–14: Links wisdom, obedience, and restoration, affirming that covenant hope continues beyond exile and apparent loss, including death itself. This passage confirms that resurrection hope remained intact even after national judgment.

Second Temple Confirmation

Hebrews 11:35: Acknowledges resurrection hope as already known and trusted among the faithful, indicating continuity rather than introduction.

Messianic Confirmation

Gospel of John 5:28–29: Yahusha affirms resurrection for both the righteous and the unrighteous, confirming established covenant teaching rather than presenting a novel doctrine.

Resurrection hope was preserved within covenant instruction long before Yahusha; He did not introduce it, but confirmed, clarified, and authoritatively affirmed it.

Read Chapter 8 **Yahuah: Restoration Guide**
Different types of calendars

Alignment Focus — Chapter 8 (Covenantal Time & Resurrection Expectation)

While **Week 10** established canonical continuity of testimony, **Week 11** clarifies that covenant hope—especially resurrection—exists within **Yahuah's appointed times,** not human-altered systems of chronology.

Chapter 8 from **Yahuah: Restoration Guide**, students are to extract the following **specific emphases for Week 11:**

- **Resurrection Is Anchored in Appointed Times:** Chapter 8 demonstrates that Yahuah governs history through fixed times, seasons, and epochs, not arbitrary human calendars. Resurrection hope is therefore covenantal and scheduled within divine order, not philosophical speculation.

- **Human Calendars Alter Structure, Not Promise:** The chapter documents how empires altered calendars, feast dates, and week structures. Despite this, covenant promises—including restoration and resurrection—were **never nullified,** only obscured. This supports Hebrews 11:35, which testifies that resurrection hope existed **before** later doctrinal systems.

- **Covenant Hope Survives Chronological Corruption:** Chapter 8 confirms that even when holy days, Shabbath, and months were confused, **doctrinal hope remained intact.** Baruch's promise of restoration and Yahusha's declaration in John 5 operate within this preserved covenant framework.

- **Resurrection Belongs to Yahuah's Order, Not Institutional Time:** By establishing that the biblical day begins at **dawn,** not midnight or sunset, Chapter 8 reinforces that life, restoration, and resurrection follow **creation order,** not Roman or ecclesiastical constructs.

This clarifies why resurrection doctrine could be preserved accurately even when calendars were corrupted.

KEY TERMS AND DEFINITIONS (WEEK 11)

- Resurrection: The divinely enacted restoration of life following death, affirming that covenant faithfulness, obedience, and righteousness are not nullified by mortality but are preserved for future renewal and judgment according to Yahuah's purpose.

- Covenant Hope: The sustained expectation of restoration, vindication, and renewal grounded in Yahuah's covenant promises, preserved across generations through faithful instruction and confirmed through historical and prophetic witness.

- Doctrinal Continuity: The faithful transmission of covenant belief and instruction across time without contradiction, demonstrating consistency of divine purpose despite changes in administration, historical context, or mode of revelation.

COVENANTAL STUDY TASK

Pause your reading and complete the following before proceeding. Engage the Scriptural text directly. Do not summarize secondary opinions.

- ***Trace resurrection hope across preserved covenant writings***
- ***Distinguish doctrinal continuity from historical or calendrical alteration***

FINAL THOUGHTS ON WEEK 11

"Resurrection hope was preserved before it was proclaimed."

QUOTE REFLECTION

"Hope preserved becomes truth revealed."

TERM I - MONTH 3 — WEEK 12 - COVENANT LANGUAGE UNITY

ONE YADA YAHUAH (THEOLOGY), THROUGH CONSISTENT COVENANT LANGUAGE - ONE LANGUAGE ONE

Week 12 Learning Outcomes — Covenant Language Unity

By the end of Week 12, students should be able to:

- Define covenant language unity and explain why meaning preservation safeguards doctrine
- Identify covenant terms that remain consistent across centuries and writings
- Distinguish unchanged vocabulary from distorted practice or institutional redefinition
- Demonstrate continuity of meaning across Apokryfos, Prophets, Yahusha's teaching, and emissary writings

PURPOSE OF WEEK 12

To demonstrate that doctrinal unity is preserved through consistent language and meaning across generations.

TERM I - MONTH 3 - WEEK 12 - READING

- **Tobit 12:6–10:** Defines righteousness, prayer, and charity using covenant language.
- **Enoch 22:1–4:** Describes post-death separation using structured covenant categories.
- **Daniel 12:2:** Defines resurrection outcomes.
- **Luke 16:19–31:** Yahusha uses existing covenant language to explain accountability.
- **James 1:27:** Defines pure worship in covenantal terms.

Read Chapter 9 Yahuah: Restoration Guide

ALIGNMENT FOCUS — CHAPTER 9

Chapter 9 demonstrates that despite persecution, corruption, exile, and violence, the covenant language itself remains unchanged.

The persecutors change systems, names, calendars, and institutions, but they do not succeed in altering the meaning of covenant terms.

From Chapter 9, students are to extract the following specific emphases for Week 12:

- **Persecution Does Not Alter Doctrinal Language**

  Those who persecuted the followers of YAHUAH sought to suppress obedience, Shabbath, feasts, and covenant practice, yet the vocabulary of righteousness, idolatry, repentance, judgment, and restoration remained intact across generations.

This confirms covenant language unity under pressure.

- **False Authority Preserves Language While Distorting Practice**

  Chapter 9 shows that persecutors often retained covenant terms while redefining behavior.

  This reinforces the necessity of distinguishing words from meaning, a core principle of covenant language unity.

- **Covenant Terms Retain Meaning Across Judgment and Hope**

  The same covenant language used to describe persecution, idolatry, judgment, resurrection, and restoration appears consistently in Tobit, Enoch, Daniel, Yahusha's teachings, and the emissaries.

  Meaning is preserved even when circumstances change.

- **Idolatry as a Covenant Constant**

  Chapter 9 defines idolatry using consistent Hebrew terms and biblical definitions.

  This confirms that covenant vocabulary regarding false worship, obedience, and judgment never evolves culturally—it remains doctrinally fixed.

Truth does not change languages; it preserves meaning.

KEY TERMS AND DEFINITIONS (WEEK 12)

- Covenant Language Unity: The consistent use and preservation of covenant vocabulary across Scriptural writings, ensuring that core theological meanings remain unified rather than fragmented by time, language, or context.
- Yada Yahuah (Theological) Term: A word or phrase that carries defined covenant meaning, shaping how Yahuah, His instruction, and His purposes are understood. Theological terms function as carriers of doctrine, not merely descriptive language.
- Continuity of Meaning: The faithful preservation of covenant doctrine through language, in which key terms retain their intended meaning across generations, writings, and administrations without contradiction.

COVENANTAL STUDY TASK

Pause your reading and complete the following before proceeding. Engage the Scriptural text directly. Do not summarize secondary opinions.

- *Trace covenant language across the assigned writings*
- *Distinguish preserved meaning from distorted practice or redefinition*

FINAL THOUGHTS ON WEEK 12

"One covenant speaks with one voice."

QUOTE REFLECTION

"Truth preserves meaning across generations."

ASSESSMENT ALIGNMENT — MONTH 3

Each week of Month 3 contributes directly to the student's ability to defend continuity without innovation:

- Week 9 establishes the governing principle of concealment and timed revelation
- Week 10 demonstrates canonical continuity through preserved intertextual witness
- Week 11 confirms doctrinal continuity of resurrection hope across covenants
- Week 12 establishes covenant language unity as a safeguard of doctrinal meaning

Students must integrate concealment, continuity, doctrine, and language into a single covenant argument by the end of the month.

CORE CONCEPTS TO RE-ANCHOR

Students must be able to clearly articulate and retain the following foundational principles before advancing:

- **Concealment vs. Rejection (Week 9)**
  - Concealment is an act of divine governance, not loss or error.
  - Yahuah determines when truth is revealed and to whom.
  - Apokryfos writings were preserved, not discarded.
- **Canonical Continuity (Week 10)**
  - The Renewed Covenant reveals, it does not invent.
  - The "righteous sufferer" theme existed before Yahusha's ministry.
  - Apokryfos function as a Covenantal Bridge, not an alternative canon.
- **Doctrinal Preservation Across Time (Week 11)**
  - Resurrection hope predates the Renewed Covenant.
  - Calendar corruption and human systems do not nullify covenant promises.
  - Doctrine survives even when structure and timing are altered.

- **Covenant Language (Week 12)**
    - Covenant truth is preserved through consistent meaning, not language uniformity.
    - Yahusha and the emissaries speak using existing covenant vocabulary.
    - Yada Yahuah (Theology) is transmitted through shared definitions, not innovation.

STUDENT SELF-ASSESSMENT CHECKLIST

By the end of Month 3, the student should be able to:

- Explain why "hidden" writings can still be covenant-faithful
- Identify continuity between Apokryfos and Renewed Covenant texts
- Defend resurrection doctrine as pre-existing, not newly introduced
- Recognize shared Yada Yahuah (theological) language across centuries
- Distinguish preservation from institutional canonization

Guiding Statement for Month 3

What Yahuah preserves, time cannot erase; what He conceals, He later reveals.

TERM I: MONTH 4
COVENANT SALVATION

Grace Through Faith, Resurrection, and Covenant Citizenship

WEEK 13 LEARNING OUTCOMES — COVENANT SALVATION

By the end of Week 13, students should be able to:

- Defend salvation as a covenant reality grounded in grace through faith from the earliest Scriptural witness
- Explain the Scriptural order of death (sleep), resurrection, judgment, and eternal outcome
- Distinguish covenant obedience as evidence of faithfulness rather than a means of earning salvation
- Demonstrate how Yahusha confirms and fulfills established covenant salvation rather than introducing a new system

Read Chapter 10 **Yahuah: Restoration Guide**

Purpose of Week 13

To confirm that salvation has always been by grace through faith, and to establish the covenant order of death (sleep), resurrection, judgment, and eternal outcome as taught consistently in Scripture.

Term I - Month 4 - Week 13 — Reading

- **Ephesians 2:8–9:** Salvation is by grace through faith, not by works.
- **Habakkuk 2:4**: The righteous live by faith.
- **John 14:6:** Yahusha is the only way to the Father (Yahuah).
- **Acts 16:30–31:** Believe in the Master Yahusha the Mashiyach and you will be saved.
- **John 11:11:** Death is described as sleep.

- **John 5:28–29:** All in the graves will hear His voice—resurrection of life or resurrection of condemnation.
- **Matthew 25:46:** Eternal punishment vs eternal life.
- **Ecclesiastes (Qoheleth) 9:5–6:** The dead know nothing; no participation in what is done under the sun.
- **1 Thessalonians 4:16–17:** The dead in Messiah rise first; the living are caught up to meet Yahusha in the air.
- **Revelation 20:4–6:** Reign with Mashiyach a thousand years; blessed are those in the first resurrection.
- **Revelation 20:14–15:** Second death; lake of fire; only those written in the Book of Life remain.
- **Philippians 3:21:** The righteous receive transformed bodies like His glorious body.
- **Revelation 21:2:** New Yerushalayim comes down from heaven, prepared as a bride.
- **Matthew 24:13:** He who endures to the end will be saved.
- **John 8:51:** If a man keeps My saying, he shall never see death.
- **John 14:15:** If you love Me, keep My commandments.
- **John 5:39**: The Scriptures testify of Yahusha.
- **Tehillim 119:15–16:** Meditate in His precepts; delight in His statutes; do not forget His word.
- **Joshua 1:8:** Meditate day and night; observe to do; then prosperity and success.
- **1 Thessalonians 5:17:** Pray without ceasing.

Alignment Focus — Chapter 10 (Salvation & Covenant Order)
While previous weeks established doctrinal continuity and resurrection hope, Week 13 brings these threads together by clarifying salvation as a unified covenant reality rather than a fragmented or evolving concept.

From Chapter 10 of *Yahuah: Restoration Guide,* students are to extract the following emphases for Week 13:

- Salvation Is Covenantal, Not Transactional: Chapter 10 demonstrates that salvation has always been initiated by Yahuah's grace and received through faith, never purchased by works or ritual performance. Obedience functions as covenant loyalty, not as currency.
- Faith Produces Citizenship, Not Mere Belief: The chapter emphasizes that faith is relational and covenantal, resulting in allegiance, perseverance, and transformed living rather than intellectual assent alone.
- Salvation Follows Divine Order, Not Human Assumption: Chapter 10 confirms the Scriptural sequence of death as sleep, resurrection, judgment, and eternal outcome, correcting assumptions of immediate reward or punishment after death.
- Yahusha Confirms the Covenant Pattern of Salvation: Rather than replacing prior instruction, Yahusha affirms and fulfills the covenant salvation pattern already present in Torah, the Prophets, and the Writings.

Key Terms and Definitions (Week 13)

- Salvation: The covenantal act of deliverance and restoration accomplished by Yahuah through Yahusha, rescuing the faithful from judgment and corruption and restoring them to right standing and purpose within the covenant.
- Grace: The unearned favor and active intervention of Elohiym that initiates rescue, sustains restoration, and empowers covenant faithfulness, rather than excusing disobedience or nullifying instruction.
- Faith: Covenantal trust in Yahuah that results in loyalty, obedience, and perseverance, demonstrated through faithful action rather than mere belief or verbal confession.
- Resurrection: The divinely enacted restoration of life after death, through which the righteous are vindicated and the unrighteous are judged, affirming covenant accountability and eternal destiny.
- Book of Life: The covenantal record of those who belong to Yahuah through faithfulness, obedience, and allegiance to Yahusha, representing divine

acknowledgment rather than arbitrary inclusion.

- New Yarushalayim: The promised dwelling place of Yahuah with the righteous, depicted as descending to earth, where covenant restoration, righteousness, and divine presence are fully realized rather than escaped from creation.

COVENANTAL STUDY TASK

Pause your reading and complete the following before proceeding. Engage the Scriptural text directly. Do not summarize secondary opinions.

• Identify the unchanging foundation of salvation (grace through faith).

• Identify the Scriptural order:

death (sleep) → resurrection → judgment → eternal outcome.

• Identify the covenant signs of citizenship in the Kingdom (obedience as evidence, not purchase).

FINAL THOUGHTS ON WEEK 13

"Salvation has never changed—grace through faith is the covenant foundation."

QUOTE REFLECTION

"Hope is not invented in the Renewed Covenant; it is fulfilled in Yahusha."

TERM I: MONTH 4
QUALIFICATION & INTEGRATION MONTH
FOUNDATIONS OF CANON & RESTORATION
ACADEMIC ORIENTATION — TERM I · MONTH 4 – WEEK 14

Week 14 - 16 functions as a qualification and integration period, not an instructional unit. No new doctrinal material is introduced. Instead, students are evaluated on their ability to synthesize, articulate, and apply the restored covenantal framework established in Weeks 1-13.

THIS MONTH VERIFIES WHETHER THE STUDENT HAS DEVELOPED:
•Covenantal Reasoning discipline
•Faithfulness to the restored Yada Yahuah (theological) method
•Competence in Scripture-based academic writing
•Conceptual clarity and terminological precision

Month 4 is evaluative by design. Advancement is conditional. Students are expected to demonstrate mastery, not exploration.

Month 4 is the qualification and integration month for Term I — Foundations of Canon & Restoration.

Methodological Fidelity — Evaluation Standard
All assessments in Month 4 are evaluated according to the restored Yada Yahuah (theological) method established in Term I. This method includes:
* **Scripture as Self-Defining Authority**
  Scriptural Witness is derived from Scriptural testimony, not institutional validation.
* **Covenantal Reasoning**

Authority, preservation, and doctrine are evaluated through covenantal appointment, not popularity or tradition.

- **Continuity Without Innovation**
  Fulfillment is understood as completion, not replacement or doctrinal invention.
- **Textual and Covenant Language Precision**
  Doctrinal meaning is preserved through consistent covenant language and accurate textual handling.
- **Restricted Source Discipline**
  Only assigned Scriptural texts and Term I materials are permitted. External theological systems are excluded.

Deviation from this method constitutes methodological failure regardless of essay length or stylistic quality.

No new instructional content is introduced by the end of this this month.
Instead, the student is required to demonstrate comprehension, integration, and academic discipline based on the material studied in Months 1–3.

MODULE 4 LEARNING OUTCOMES

By the end of Term I – Month 4, the student must be able to:

- Synthesize Scriptural Witness, preservation, and continuity into a coherent Scriptural framework
- Demonstrate disciplined use of Scripture without reliance on institutional Yada Yahuah (theology)
- Explain how translation, guardianship, and restored authority affect doctrine
- Apply restored Yada Yahuah (theology) consistently across multiple topics
- Use precise covenant terminology with conceptual accuracy
- Produce structured academic writing aligned with Institute standards

Successful demonstration of these outcomes is required for advancement to

Stage II.

This month evaluates whether the student has:
- understood restored Scriptural Witness
- grasped Scriptural preservation and guardianship
- adopted a restored Yada Yahuah (theological) method
- developed basic academic writing competence

Successful completion of Month 4 is required to advance to Stage II (Master-Level Studies).

REQUIRED SOURCES (ALL WEEKS)

All work must be completed using:
- Dabar Yahuah Scriptures
- Dabar Yahuah Bible App
- Assigned readings from Term I

No external theological systems, devotional materials, or denominational sources are permitted.

MONTH 4 ESSAY — INTEGRATIVE CAPSTONE"
TERM I: MONTH 4 — WEEK 14
Week 14 Learning Outcomes

BY THE END OF WEEK 14, THE STUDENT MUST BE ABLE TO:
- Integrate material from Months 1–3 into a unified canonical argument
- Explain how Scripture defines its own authority and preservation
- Analyze the doctrinal impact of translation history using Scriptural evidence
- Demonstrate progression of understanding across the term
- Produce a structured Yada Yahuah (theological) analysis using Scripture alone

INTEGRATIVE CAPSTONE ESSAY
Title: Canon, Translation, and Restored Authority
Length: 2,000–3,000 words

Purpose of the Essay
This essay serves as the single integrative assessment for Term I.

The student must demonstrate the ability to:
- synthesize material from Months 1–3
- reason canonically using Scripture alone
- explain how translation, preservation, and authority affect doctrine

This is not a personal testimony or devotional reflection.
It is a structured Yada Yahuah (theological) analysis.
Essay Focus

Explain how:
- Scripture defines its own authority
- priestly guardianship preserved canonical integrity

- translation history (including the removal of the Sacred Name) affected doctrine
- restored Scripture corrects doctrinal confusion

The essay must show progression of understanding from Month 1 through

Month 3.

Required Scripture (Minimum Use)

Students must meaningfully engage with the following passages:

- Shemoth 3:13–15
- Tehillim 83:18
- Hosea 12:9
- Matthew 4:4
- Revelation 22:18–19

Additional Scriptures from Term I are expected where relevant.

Evaluation Criteria (Applies to Final Essay)

The essay will be evaluated on:

- Sc**riptural accuracy**
- **Covenantal Reasoning**
- **Conceptual clarity**
- **Logical structure**
- **Faithf**ulness to restored Yada Yahuah (theological) method

TERM I: MONTH 4 — WEEK 15

Terminology Mastery — Foundational Competency Verification

This component verifies that the student has internalized the vocabulary required for restored Yada Yahuah (theological) study. Mastery is demonstrated through understanding and correct application, not memorization. Terminology functions as a doctrinal framework. Inability to define or apply these terms accurately indicates insufficient readiness for advanced study.

Week 15 Learning Outcomes — Terminology Mastery Summary

By the end of Week 15, the student must be able to:

- Define core covenant terms with precision and clarity
- Explain the functional role of each term within restored Yada Yahuah (theology)
- Identify how misunderstanding terminology leads to doctrinal error
- Demonstrate internalization of vocabulary rather than rote memorization

TERMINOLOGY MASTERY SUMMARY

Title: *Foundations of Canon & Restoration*

Format: Structured list with brief explanations

Length: Flexible (recommended 500–800 words total)

Purpose

This component verifies that the student has internalized the vocabulary necessary for restored Yada Yahuah (theological) study.

Students must demonstrate understanding, not memorization.

Required Terminology (Minimum Coverage)

Students must define and explain key terms from Months 1–4, including but not limited to:

- Dabar / Dabar Yahuah
- Tôrâh (Instruction vs Law)
- Canon (Divine vs Institutional)
- Apokryfos
- Concealment vs Revelation
- Priesthood (Levitical vs Malkîy-Tsedeq)
- Guardianship
- Sacred Name
- Restored Yada Yahuah (theology)
- Doctrinal Continuity

Each term must include:

- a clear definition
- its function within restored Yada Yahuah (theology)
- why misunderstanding this term causes doctrinal error

TERM I: MONTH 4 — WEEK 16
Week 16 Learning Outcomes — Final Submission & Advancement Review

By the end of Week 16, the student must be able to:
- Submit all required work according to Institute academic standards
- Demonstrate consistency of method, terminology, and reasoning
- Meet qualification criteria for advancement without remediation

FINAL SUBMISSION & ADVANCEMENT REVIEW
SUBMISSION EXPECTATIONS
All submissions must follow these academic standards:
- Scriptural citations only
- Clear structure and progression
- No devotional language
- No denominational appeals
- No speculative Yada Yahuah (theology)

The goal is demonstrated understanding, not persuasion.
Assessment Alignment — Qualification Threshold

Month 4 evaluates competency, not participation. Advancement decisions are based on demonstrated mastery of Term I foundations.

Satisfactory Performance Includes:
- Accurate Scriptural reasoning
- Faithful application of restored Yada Yahuah (theological) method
- Clear structural organization and logical progression

- Correct use of covenant terminology
- Compliance with source and methodology restrictions

Unsatisfactory Performance Includes:
- Reliance on external theological systems
- Doctrinal inconsistency or contradiction
- Methodological deviation
- Vague or imprecise terminology
- Failure to integrate Months 1–3 coherently

Only students meeting satisfactory criteria may proceed to Stage II.

ADVANCEMENT DECISION

At the conclusion of Month 4, faculty will issue one of the following:
- Satisfactory — Advancement Approved
- Unsatisfactory — Remediation Required

Only students who receive Satisfactory may proceed to Stage II (Master-Level Studies).

ACADEMIC PROGRAM STRUCTURE

Yahuah Institute of Biblical Restoration, Inc.

STAGE I — ASSOCIATE-LEVEL FOUNDATIONS

Status: ✓ Completed upon satisfactory evaluation

This confirms foundational competency in:
- Scriptural Witness
- Scriptural preservation
- Restored Yada Yahuah (theological) method
- Academic analysis

Students who complete Stage I are eligible to apply for Stage II.

Remarks:

It is a mandatory submission requirement.

The structure finalized makes it unmistakable:

Month 4 is a qualification month

- Advancement is conditional
- The Capstone Essay is the single integrative assessment
- Failure to submit = failure to advance

A student must clearly understand that:

1. They must submit an essay (2,000–3,000 words)
2. The essay evaluates Months 1–3
3. Scripture use is required, not suggested
4. Methodology is restricted
5. The outcome directly affects advancement to Stage II

End of Term I — Qualification Complete

Completion of Month 4 signifies fulfillment of **Stage I — Associate-Level Foundations.** Advancement to Stage II is contingent upon satisfactory evaluation of all Month 4 requirements.

No student may proceed without formal approval.

CONCLUSION — BOOK 1 ↦ BOOK 2

The first stage of the Master of Biblical Restoration Studies has established the necessary foundation: that Dabar Yahuah originates with Yahuah, is preserved in heaven, transmitted through covenantal guardianship, and restored through Yadaʿ Yahuah rather than speculative theology (Yada Yahuah). Authority has been correctly reordered. Canon has been re-anchored. Tradition has been placed beneath instruction. Covenant continuity has been clarified.
Yet foundation alone is not completion.

Having established where instruction originates, how it is preserved, and who is authorized to guard it, the student must now advance to the next level of covenantal reasoning. The second stage moves beyond foundational authority into the development of covenant structure, priestly administration, covenant identity, and the formation of disciplined interpretive mastery.

MBRS Book 2 therefore transitions the student from Associate-Level foundations into Bachelor-Level covenant development — where restored authority is no longer merely understood, but systematically applied.
The journey from knowing that Dabar is true now advances into learning how Dabar governs all covenant life.

TERM I — GLOSSARY

Accountability: The obligation to answer for actions taken within or beyond one's assigned authority.

Agency: The responsible actor behind an action or outcome.

Alignment: Harmony between human action and divine instruction within established order. Gradual reordering under divine authority rather than instantaneous perfection. Agreement between renewed desire and divine instruction flowing from new nature.

Awareness: Moral perception gained without participation in evil or alteration of created nature.

Boundary: A limit that enables purpose and jurisdiction rather than restriction. The point where mercy's invitation ends and restoration is protected through enforcement.

Boundary Violation: The willful crossing of an assigned limit with knowledge of prohibition. Targeting prohibited realms, unions, or acts that corrupt order

Capacity: The ability to receive covenant, correction, and restoration.

Completion: The declared state of lacking nothing within the creation week sequence.

Condition: The internal spiritual and biological state that governs and shapes human existence, from which outward behavior, capacity, alignment, and manifestation proceed. Condition reflects origin and nature, not merely action, and determines how life is expressed in the physical realm.

Containment: The maintenance of order through enforced boundaries that prevent the spread or escalation of corruption. Divine limitation or removal designed to preserve creation. Covenantal removal of embodied rebellion. Divine restraint that limits spread while postponing final eradication. Divine restraint that limits spread while preserving agency. Removal of irreparable corruption to prevent return and preserve restoration.

Expulsion: Protective restriction of access to prevent eternal corruption.

Firmament: The divinely structured expanse established by Yahuah that contains and orders the created world. The firmament encompasses the earth in its entirety, the first heaven (the sky), and functions as the structural boundary separating the waters below from the waters above. It is the framework within which land, sea, sky, luminaries, life, and human habitation are set in place. The firmament is not merely atmospheric space, but the heavenly structure of the world as created, defining realms, limits, and functions by divine command. It establishes order, containment, and stability, ensuring that creation operates within assigned boundaries until the appointed time of restoration.

Foundational Order: That which is established first and therefore governs all later interpretation.

Kind: A divinely fixed boundary established by Yahuah to preserve created order, identity, and lawful reproduction. Each kind is created according to its own nature, function, and capacity, and reproduction is permitted only within that assigned boundary. Mixing of kinds is prohibited because it violates creational design and produces disorder rather than life.

The creation of **Adam and Eve—male and female, distinct yet complementary—**demonstrates that continuity and fruitfulness depend on ordered distinction, not mixture. Any attempt to merge kinds—whether biologically, spiritually, or instructionally—constitutes rebellion against Yahuah's design and results in corruption rather than preservation.

Knowledge of Evil: Awareness gained through transgression, not divine creation.

Order: Divine structure, assignment, and boundary established at creation.

Procreation: The gift uniquely granted to humanity to preserve life in mortality.

Separation: Division established by Yahuah to preserve order, function, and life. A deliberate, redemptive distinction established to preserve purity and continuity. Termination of a prior claim enabling covenant transfer. The final protective act that secures restored creation once alignment is complete.

Shabbâth: The sanctified seventh day established by Yahuah at creation as a covenantal sign of completion, authority, and alignment. Shabbâth was set apart in the very first week of creation, not as a human ordinance, but as a divine marker that creation had reached its intended order and rest under Yahuah's sovereignty. Shabbâth functions as a signal of covenant relationship between Yahuah and His chosen—celebrated by Yahuah Himself in heaven, by the Angels of the Presence and the Angels of the Sanctification, and by those on earth whom Yahuah has sanctified and set apart. It is not given to all nations indiscriminately, but to those brought into covenant alignment and sanctification. Shabbâth testifies that authority, time, and completion belong to Yahuah alone. To keep Shabbâth is to acknowledge Yahuah as Creator, Sustainer, and Covenant King, and to reject competing systems that redefine time, labor, worship, or rest. It is therefore both a creational ordinance and a living covenant sign, preserved across ages as a witness of sanctification and belonging.

Testing: A permitted process that reveals faithfulness without originating evil

Tree of Life: The source of sustained immortality, withheld to preserve redemption.

www.ingramcontent.com/pod-product-compliance
Lightning Source LLC
Chambersburg PA
CBHW080608090426
42735CB00017B/3367